■ SCHOLASTIC

Reteaching Math

MULTIPLICATION & DIVISION

Mini-Lessons, Games & Activities to Review & Reinforce Essential Math Concepts & Skills

Audrey Kennan & Bob Krech

New York • Toronto • London • Auckland • Sydney
Mexico City • New Delhi • Hong Kong • Buenos Aires

Teaching *Resources*

DEDICATION

To the Mathematicians of Room 211—
past, present, and future.
—AK

ACKNOWLEDGMENTS

Thank you, Bob Krech, for inviting me to join this fun math project.
Thank you, Mathemagician Suzanne Drennon, for believing an English major could do math.
—AK

Thanks to Maria Chang and Deborah Schecter
for all the opportunities and support.
—BK

Editor: Maria L. Chang
Cover design by Brian LaRossa
Interior design by Holly Grundon
Interior illustrations by Mike Moran

ISBN-13: 978-0-439-52967-9
ISBN-10: 0-439-52967-0
Copyright © 2008 by Bob Krech
All rights reserved.
Printed in the U.S.A.

1 2 3 4 5 6 7 8 9 10   40   15 14 13 12 11 10 09 08

Table of Contents

Table of Contents (continued)

REPRODUCIBLE STUDENT PAGES

Introduction

Most math books that have the word *reteaching* in the title typically feature many pages of equations and practice problems. The reasoning may be that if students require a concept or skill to be retaught, the best way for them to gain mastery is to practice more of the same. Research does show that some students need more time on a task than other students in order to learn a concept. However, if a student does not understand a concept or skill the first time, presenting a series of problems that the student already finds difficult and repeating them, without new knowledge or intervention, will most likely not be successful.

To reteach implies actually teaching again, not merely repeated practice. Students need to have a strong conceptual understanding if they are going to be able to do mathematics with accuracy and comprehension. Without this understanding, math can become meaningless and students simply work by rote. That's why we've created the Reteaching Math series. You will find this series is different from most reteaching books in that the emphasis is on helping students develop understanding as well as providing useful practice.

Using a Problem-Solving Approach

The activities, games, and lessons in this book are just plain good instruction, with an emphasis on solving problems and applying math in context. Problem solving is the first process standard listed in the NCTM *Principles and Standards for School Mathematics* (2000). The accompanying statement reads, "Problem solving should be the central focus of all mathematics instruction and an integral part of all mathematical activity." In other words, problem solving is what math is all about. Every lesson here begins with a problem to solve to help create a spirit of inquiry and interest. Practice problems are integrated into the lessons so they are meaningful. Real reteaching!

Providing Context

It is important to provide students with a context to help give learning mathematical skills and concepts meaning. Context helps learners understand how these mathematical ideas and tools are useful and can be applied to real-life problems and situations. Context can be provided by creating a theme that carries throughout all the lessons. In this book, the theme of Cardenza's Collector Card and Coin Company provides a context in which learning about multiplication and division is relevant, motivating, and fun. A generous dose of humor is included to help ease the anxiety many students feel over multiplication and division in particular, and math in general. The use of the overarching Card and Coin Company theme gives all the lessons a sense of cohesion, purpose, and interest.

Addressing Various Learning Styles

A good way to help all students learn mathematics well is to present ideas through physical, pictorial, and symbolic representations. Research suggests the importance of learning math ideas through modeling with manipulatives. Math concepts need to be experienced on a physical level before pictorial and more abstract representations can be truly understood. Relying completely on symbolic representations (e.g., lots of equations) is rarely enough, particularly in a reteaching situation.

Learning experiences featured here include using manipulatives, drawing pictures, writing equations, reading stories, and playing games to help learners gain a strong conceptual knowledge.

What's Inside?

Activity Lessons – introduce major concepts and skills. Timed to last about 40 minutes, these lessons are designed to help students work on the ideas in a hands-on manner and context to help them understand the meaning behind the math and give them an opportunity to apply it in a fun way.

Practice Pages – specially designed to provide both practice and a helpful reference sheet for students. Each practice page begins with a word problem so students can see how and why the math is useful in solving real problems. Each page also features a **Basics Box**. Here, concepts are carefully presented with words, numbers, pictures, definitions, and step-by-step explanations. **Example problems** help solidify understanding, then a series of problems give students practice. Finally, a **journal prompt** helps students discuss and explore the concept using pictures, numbers, and words, while providing you an assessment opportunity that looks at student thinking and understanding. Practice pages can be worked on together in class, assigned to be done independently, or given as homework assignments.

Review Pages – provide students with additional focused practice on a specific math concept. The concept is practiced in a variety of formats and is designed to be completed independently. In addition, a **mixed review** of concepts introduced earlier is included in many review pages. By spiraling the curriculum in this way, students' retention and recall of math ideas is supported. These pages may be used for review, practice, homework, or assessment of students' knowledge and understanding.

How to Use This Book

This book can be used as a replacement unit, as a resource for activities for math workshops or centers, or as a supplement to find engaging ideas to enhance a textbook unit. The lessons and activities are presented in a developmental sequence, but can be used as stand-alone or supplementary learning experiences. Since it's written to accommodate all learners you can use it to teach a unit on multiplication and division to any class.

About Multiplication and Division

Multiplication and division are operations that ultimately help us answer the question, "How many?" Multiplication centers on determining how many there are in all when counting groups of the same size. Meanwhile, division helps us determine how a number of items can be divided up into same-size groups or how many groups there could be with a given number of items, and how many items might be in a group. The two operations are closely related both in meaning and mechanics.

Multiplication and division are discussed in the NCTM Standards under the Number and Operations Standard. The expectations for grades 4–6 include:

- understand various meanings of multiplication and division
- understand the effects of multiplying and dividing whole numbers
- identify and use relationships between operations, such as division as the inverse of multiplication, to solve problems
- understand the properties of operations, such as the distributivity of multiplication over addition
- develop fluency with basic number combinations for multiplication and division and use these combinations to mentally compute related problems such as 30 x 50
- develop fluency in multiplying and dividing whole numbers
- develop and use strategies to estimate the results of whole-number computations and to judge the reasonableness of such results

- select appropriate methods and tools for computing with whole numbers from among mental computation, estimation, calculators, and paper and pencil, according to the context and nature of the computation, and use the selected method or tool

Within these expectations are more specific objectives. These are addressed in the learning experiences throughout this book and include:

- understand how arrays model multiplication
- learn a variety of strategies to help with basic multiplication facts
- understand and apply the commutative property of multiplication
- use multiplication patterns to solve problems
- multiply multi-digit numbers
- divide with and without remainders
- divide with a single-digit divisor
- divide with multi-digit divisors

Part 1: Multiplication

Materials

- 36 counting manipulatives (e.g., chips, cubes)
- *Amanda Bean's Amazing Dream* (see "Literature Link" below)
- Practice Page #1 (p. 36)
- Review Page #1 (p. 37)

Literature Link

Amanda Bean's Amazing Dream by Cindy Neuschwander (Scholastic, 1998)

In this fun-to-use picture book, Amanda Bean loves to count anything and everything. She counts constantly until she has an amazing dream in which she discovers the benefits of multiplication. There are lots of good picture examples where multiplication is very useful in determining the number of items in the picture.

ACTIVITY LESSON #1

From Addition to Multiplication
(INTRODUCING MULTIPLICATION)

> **Overview:** Students learn how multiplication is similar to repeated addition and how it is an efficient way to find out "how many."

Prepare for the class by putting out six groups of six manipulatives on the floor. Invite students to join you in a circle around the manipulatives. Say, "Take a look at these and see if you can tell how many there are. I'm going to ask you in about a minute, but when you tell me, I also want you to tell me how you figured it out." Give students time to develop an answer, then ask for responses. (Some students will count by sixes, some will count by twos, some will count by ones, and some will multiply 6×6.)

Tell the class, "There are many ways to figure out how many counters there are here. Some methods are more efficient than others. *Efficient* means 'quick and accurate.' Counting by ones might be accurate, but it is not quick. Counting by sixes is quicker and probably more accurate, but knowing the multiplication fact 6×6 is quickest and most efficient of all. If we organize a set of items into groups of the same number of items, this helps us to use repeated addition or multiplication." Draw a few examples of this idea on the board.

Explain that one of the reasons we learn to memorize multiplication facts is because it is a very efficient way to find out "how many" in lots of situations. Tell students that you're going to read a book that tells about a girl who didn't believe learning multiplication facts was a very important skill until she had an amazing dream.

Read aloud *Amanda Bean's Amazing Dream*. Stop at various points in the book as Amanda tries to determine the number of items in a sequence of her dream (e.g., wheels on the bicycles, balls of yarn, etc.) and have students take turns figuring out how many of the item there are.

Choose an example from the book, such as the scene in the bakery where there are 3 shelves, each shelf with 3 cakes. Draw a quick sketch of this on the board. Say, "How many ways can we write about this arrangement of cakes using number sentences?" ($3 + 3 + 3 = 9$; $3 \times 3 = 9$; $1 + 1 + 1 + 1 + 1 + 1 + 1 + 1 + 1 = 9$) Discuss these options and then focus on multiplication. Say, "We could follow Amanda Bean's idea and use multiplication to describe this arrangement. It is easy because the cakes are organized in equal groups. We have 3 groups of 3. So 3 and 3 are the *factors*. When we multiply factors, the answer is called a *product*. The product of 3 × 3 is 9. Some people remember this by saying, 'Factories make products. So factors make products.'"

Choose several more examples from the book. Sketch them on the board or simply display the book page. Have students use their journals or a piece of paper to write number sentences that correspond to the picture. Encourage the use of multiplication sentences as well as addition.

Do not accept number sentences that do not match the picture but still yield the correct product. For example, if you have a picture of 8 sheep with 5 balls of yarn each, 8 × 5 would be appropriate and would match the picture, but 4 × 10 would not, even though it yields the correct product of 40.

> Note: Before beginning Activity Lesson #2 have your students complete the activity "Which Has More?" as well as Practice Page #1.

ACTIVITY: **Which Has More?**

Make enough copies of "Which Has More?" (p. 35) for students. Introduce this activity by drawing on the board 3 circles with 5 stars in each circle and then 4 circles with 4 stars in each. Ask students: "Which has more?" (*4 circles with 4 stars*) Encourage students to explain how they know and then write the corresponding multiplication facts below each drawing. Tell students that they will have a chance to challenge others in the same way. Distribute the "Which Has More?" pages to students as well as colored pencils or crayons. Have students create two drawings on the page. Each should have the same items arranged in similar but slightly different groupings so that anyone looking at the page will have to look closely to calculate an answer. Each drawing should have a describing sentence underneath it, such as "3 circles with 5 stars" or "4 circles with 4 stars." At the bottom of the page, have students write the corresponding multiplication facts and answers. Then ask them to cover that area by taping a piece of paper over the answers. When they exchange papers with one another, students can check their answer by lifting the flap. Consider displaying these in the hall or as an interactive bulletin board.

Teaching Tip

Multiplication and Division Word Walls

As you begin studying multiplication and division keep a piece of large chart paper displayed prominently in the room or dedicate part of a bulletin board to serve as a multiplication and division word wall. When introducing terms such as *factor*, *product*, *dividend*, *divisor*, and *quotient*, write these words on the wall. Work with the class to create a good definition of each term as well as diagrams and examples for the chart. You may also want students to copy the definition into their math journals. Continue adding to and displaying the word wall throughout the unit.

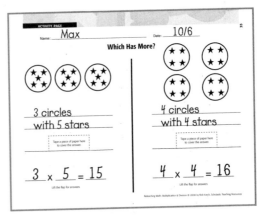

Materials

For each student:

- Letter #2 (p. 38)
- Arrays Chart (p. 39)
- pencil, colored pencils, or crayons
- 1-by-1-inch paper squares (20 for each partner group)
- Practice Page #2 (p.40)
- Review Page #2 (p. 41)

ACTIVITY LESSON #2

Cardenza's Collector Cards and Coins

(MULTIPLICATION ARRAYS)

> **Overview:** Students discover how arrays are useful ways to group elements that need to be counted and that multiplication makes finding out "how many" more efficient.

Before class starts, place copies of Letter #2 and the Arrays Chart in a large envelope addressed to the class. (Add a return address and postage if you'd like! For added fun, have a colleague deliver the envelope to your classroom.)

Hold up the envelope and invite students to predict what might be inside. Open the envelope and say, "There are copies of a letter in here, and it looks like there are enough for each of us to have one." Pass out the copies and give the class a few minutes to read the letter independently. Then invite students to take turns reading the letter aloud. Lead a discussion about the letter, making sure to clarify ideas and define any unfamiliar vocabulary.

Summarize: "So it looks like Mr. Cardenza wants us to find out how items can be arranged in different ways. These arrangements can be described by writing multiplication sentences. To do this, use paper squares, your Arrays Chart paper, and a pencil. Work with a partner to complete your paper and then we will compare results. I will assign you and your partner the number of squares to find arrays for. Let's do one together as an example."

Write the number 12 on the board. Display 12 paper squares. Ask students to suggest ways these squares can be arranged. As you arrange the squares, make a corresponding drawing for each array on the board. Then record a multiplication fact to go with it.

6×2 2×6 3×4 4×3

Have students follow the same procedure to complete their charts. Assign each pair one or two products and remind them to use only single-digit numbers or factors as they find the products. Assign these product numbers to students: 1, 2, 3, 4, 5, 6, 7, 8, 9, 10, 12, 14, 15, 16, 18, 20, 21, 24, 25, 27, 28, 30, 32, 35, 36, 40, 42, 45, 48, 49, 54, 56, 63, 64, 72, 81. When students get their numbers, have them draw their arrays on the small blank squares of their Array Charts. This activity usually takes two class periods to complete and review together.

ACTIVITY: **Human Arrays**

Here's a great way to get in some physical activity and have students create, experience, and understand arrays. Use the playground, empty cafeteria, or any large space to make multiplication arrays out of students. Some class sizes (18, 24, 30) will be easier, while some will require a discussion of remainders. Students can brainstorm: How many rows of students can we make in our class? (*2 rows of 12, 4 rows of 6, etc.*) Use a digital camera to take photos of the arrays students create, and print, label, and publish the photos in a Class Multiplication book.

Teaching Tip

Giant Array Board

After partners have completed their individual array investigations, you may want to create a Giant Array Board as a fun way to display the class findings and help summarize the discussion from the investigation. This could then serve as a class reference for multiplication and as a way to arrange and display common multiplication facts.

ACTIVITY LESSON #3

Math Secrets

(DOUBLES STRATEGY FOR MULTIPLICATION)

Overview: This lesson focuses on the concept of "Doubles" as a multiplication strategy. Students learn Doubles with relative ease and can use them to help with more difficult computation.

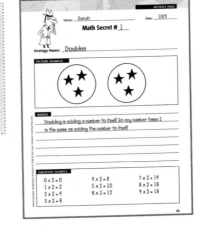

Announce to the class that you've just received another packet of letters from Mr. Cardenza. Pass out the letters and allow students to read silently, then read aloud together.

Say, "Looking over Mr. Cardenza's letter I can tell there will be a lot of math involved in helping him, particularly multiplication." Engage

Materials

For each student:

- Letter #3 (p. 42)
- Math Secret (p. 43)
- 100 Multiplication Facts Chart (p. 44)
- pencil, colored pencils or crayons
- Practice Page #3 (p. 45)
- Review Page #3 (p. 46)

Teaching Tip

Why Use Multiplication Fact Strategies?

To become proficient with basic multiplication facts, students need to develop good multiplication strategies. Memorization alone is not always sufficient. Children can memorize a fact without real understanding just as they might memorize a song in a foreign language and not know its meaning. When students learn strategies, they acquire a "math tool box" that they can rely on to help recall facts they may forget. The process and careful observation of fact patterns build their operational number sense.

Literature Link

Two of Everything
by Lily Toy Hong (Whitman, 1993)

This short picture book features a Chinese folktale in which Mr. Haktak digs up a magic pot. When he puts in 5 gold coins, they turn into 10 gold coins. One coat becomes 2. The pot doubles everything placed in it. Unfortunately, trouble results when Mrs. Haktak falls in the pot! Lots of fun and lots of doubling facts.

students in a discussion about how multiplication might be helpful in running a collector card and coin company.

Continue: "To help us with learning about multiplication, Mr. Cardenza has sent us a Math Secret page." Show a copy of this page. Say, "It looks like the first secret to work on is Doubles. What do you think a 'double' is in multiplication?" (*A number multiplied by 2 or added to itself*)

Invite students to help you list some doubles on the board. List these as students volunteer them:

$0 \times 2 = 0$	$5 \times 2 = 10$
$1 \times 2 = 2$	$6 \times 2 = 12$
$2 \times 2 = 4$	$7 \times 2 = 14$
$3 \times 2 = 6$	$8 \times 2 = 16$
$4 \times 2 = 8$	$9 \times 2 = 18$

Ask students, "How are these facts like addition?" (*Doubling a number is like adding the number to itself, so $5 \times 2 = 5 + 5$.*) Call on volunteers to list the related addition fact that goes with each multiplication double.

$0 \times 2 = 0$	$0 + 0 = 0$
$1 \times 2 = 2$	$1 + 1 = 2$
$2 \times 2 = 4$	$2 + 2 = 4$
$3 \times 2 = 6$	$3 + 3 = 6$
$4 \times 2 = 8$	$4 + 4 = 8$
$5 \times 2 = 10$	$5 + 5 = 10$
$6 \times 2 = 12$	$6 + 6 = 12$
$7 \times 2 = 14$	$7 + 7 = 14$
$8 \times 2 = 16$	$8 + 8 = 16$
$9 \times 2 = 18$	$9 + 9 = 18$

Explain to students that this pattern can help them remember these facts. Guide them to notice that each product is even and always increases by 2—this useful pattern will help them find or check products.

Continue: "From his letter, Mr. Cardenza wants us to keep a Math Secrets Handbook, which lists and explains various multiplication strategies." Pass out copies of the Math Secret page and instruct students to complete the form to start their handbook. Model on the board or on the overhead how to fill out the Math Secret page. In the top box, students should draw a picture example of the strategy. For example, to explain the Doubles strategy you might draw a picture of a group of 4 cats and another group of 4 cats for a total of 8 cats. The lines in the middle are for explaining the Doubles strategy in words. The bottom box should be used to list all the facts this strategy helps with.

Next, distribute the 100 Multiplication Facts Chart to students and explain: "To complete the 100 Multiplication Facts Chart, color in all the facts you can use with this particular strategy. Label the top of the chart with the name of the strategy; in this case, Doubles."

Have students complete these forms while you circulate and assist. When these are complete, give each student a manila folder to keep all the secrets in. Have students decorate their folder and write their name on their new Math Secrets Handbook.

ACTIVITY LESSON #4

Basketball Card Multipacks

(FIVES FACTS FOR MULTIPLICATION)

Overview: Students will learn how product patterns help in learning fives facts.

Announce that you have just received a new letter from Ricardo Cardenza. Pass out copies of Letter #4 to students. Give them time to read the letter silently before reading it aloud together. Say, "It looks like Mr. Cardenza wants us to work with fives." Write the fives facts on the board.

$5 \times 0 = 0$
$5 \times 1 = 5$
$5 \times 2 = 10$
$5 \times 3 = 15$

$5 \times 4 = 20$
$5 \times 5 = 25$
$5 \times 6 = 30$
$5 \times 7 = 35$

$5 \times 8 = 40$
$5 \times 9 = 45$

Ask the class: "Do you notice any patterns with the factors and products?" (*Students may notice that the products all end in 0 or 5.*) Next, rewrite and rearrange the facts as shown below:

$5 \times 1 = 5$
$5 \times 3 = 15$
$5 \times 5 = 25$
$5 \times 7 = 35$
$5 \times 9 = 45$

$5 \times 2 = 10$
$5 \times 4 = 20$
$5 \times 6 = 30$
$5 \times 8 = 40$

Materials

For each student:
- Letter #4 (p. 47)
- Math Secret (p. 43)
- 100 Multiplication Facts Chart (p. 44)
- Practice Page #4 (p. 49)
- Review Page #4 (p. 50)
- pencil

For each pair of students:
- pack of 50 blank index cards
- 20 envelopes
- brown paper bag

Teaching Tip

Looking for Patterns on a Hundred Chart

When examining multiplication facts it is always a good idea to help students look for patterns. Patterns help us remember sequences, and so remember multiplication facts. If a fact escapes our memory, simple patterns we notice may help us retrieve it. Skip counting through a One Hundred Chart (p. 48) is a great way to observe common multiplication fact patterns. Have students color in skip counts of twos, threes, fours, fives, and all other facts. Make sure they do a page for each fact family. They will readily see how these patterns relate directly to the products of these fact families.

Ask: "What do you notice about these products and factors now?" (*Products of fives facts that have an odd factor end in 5, while products with even factors end in 0.*)

Discuss strategies for remembering fives facts. For example, it's easy to count by fives, so counting by fives can help us remember these facts. Also, it helps to know that the facts with even numbers will have a product that ends in 0 and will be a multiple of 10. Facts with odd factors will end in 5 so we can check our answer that way as well.

Say: "Now that we've looked carefully at fives facts, I think we're ready to help Mr. Cardenza with his Insect Basketball project planning. Mr. Cardenza wants us to figure out how many Insect Basketball cards are in each multipack. A multipack is a group of packs put together. Let's pretend these index cards are Insect Basketball cards, and let's practice making multipacks."

Pair up students and distribute index cards and envelopes to each pair. Instruct math partners to put exactly 5 index cards in each envelope. On the outside of each envelope, have them write the number 5 to remind them that there are 5 cards in each pack.

When students have finished grouping their cards in envelopes, ask them to hold up one 5-pack. Ask: "How many Insect Basketball cards are in one 5-pack?" (5) "How many cards are in 1 group of 5?" (5) "So what's 1 × 5?" (5) Next, ask students to hold up three 5-packs. Ask: "How many cards are in three 5-packs?" Invite students to count by fives—5, 10, 15. "So what's 3 × 5?" (15)

Instruct math partners to pick one person to be the Mystery Multipack Packer, while the other person will be the Product Guesser. The Guesser will close his eyes while the Packer puts together multipacks. The Packer will put a certain number of 5-packs in the Multipack Bag (brown paper bag). Then the Guesser will guess how many cards are in the Multipack Bag. The answer has to be a multiple of 5. Then students switch roles.

After students have practiced for awhile, invite them to work with their partners to complete Mr. Cardenza's order chart. Go over the answers as a class when they're done.

At the conclusion of the lesson, have students complete a Math Secret sheet and a 100 Multiplication Facts Chart for this new strategy.

ACTIVITY: **Make-60 Card Game** (2 to 4 players)

To play this game, put together two sets of fives-facts multiplication flash cards. Shuffle the cards and stack them on a desk. Distribute four cards to each player. At each turn, a player tries to make a number sentence by adding or subtracting the products on his cards to get to 60. For example, if a player has 5 × 5 = 25 and 7 × 5 = 35;

25 + 35 is 60. Or, if a player has 9 × 5 = 45 and 6 × 5 = 30 and
3 × 5 = 15; 45 + 30 – 15 = 60. Players discard the cards they used to
make 60. If a player can't get to 60 with her cards, however, she'll have
to pick a card from the deck and wait for her next turn to try again.
The first player to get rid of all his cards wins.

ACTIVITY: **Hand Stamp Products**

Using large sheets of butcher paper and finger paint, have students
make fives-facts arrays by stamping their entire hand on the
paper to make sets of 5 fingers. When the paint is dry, label the hand
arrays with the related fact: 5 sets of 5 fingers = 25 fingers. This makes
a great hallway mural, which students will love creating as they get
physical with the facts. If finger paint is a problem, have students trace
their hands with markers and color in later.

. . . .

ACTIVITY LESSON #5

Cleaning the Machines

(ZEROS AND ONES FACTS FOR MULTIPLICATION)

> Overview: Students will learn how any number multiplied by
> 1 is that same number, while any number multiplied by 0 equals 0.

Tell students, "We have another letter from Mr. Cardenza. Let's take a
look together." Pass out copies of Letter #5 to students. Allow students
to read silently, then read the letter aloud together.

Pair up students and ask them to fill in the Machine Cleaning chart
on the letter. When students are done, discuss their responses. Display
a transparency of the letter on the overhead and fill in the chart with
their answers. Ask students: "What did you notice about the cards
stuck in the machines? Were there a lot of cards?" (*No, there was
mostly just 1 card or 0 or some small number.*)

Say, "I noticed in several cases there were no cards in a machine.
How did you write that?" (*0*) "And so if you had 3 machines and each
machine was clear, with 0 cards stuck in it, how many cards were
stuck in that section of machines?" (*0*) "So, if you are multiplying a
number by 0, what answer will you get every time?" (*0*)

Materials

. . . .

For each student:
- Letter #5 (p. 51)
- 2 copies of Math Secret (p. 43)
- 2 copies of 100 Multiplication
  Facts Chart (p. 44)
- Practice Page #5 (p. 52)
- Review Page #5 (p. 53)
- pencil

For teacher:
- Transparency of Letter #5
- overhead markers

Teaching Tip

Using Kidpix® and Kidspiration®

Kidpix (The Learning Company) and Kidspiration (Inspiration Software) are two software programs used widely in elementary schools. They lend themselves well to some creative uses in math class, too. Have students illustrate multiplication word problems in Kidpix, drawing pictures to show groups of objects. This is quicker than the usual drawing process and the results look great. The webbing capabilities of Kidspiration are also useful for reinforcing the "groups of objects" concept. For example, put the fact product in the center of the web, then illustrate groups of items in the bubbles connected to the product. Just the motivating force of doing it on the computer and having it look so professional get kids excited about practicing multiplication with these programs.

Literature Link

2 x 2 = Boo!: A Set of Spooky Multiplication Stories
by Loreen Leedy
(Holiday House, 1995)

Multiplication facts and strategies are featured in a fun, spooky cartoon context. This picture book focuses on the times tables from 0 to 5. It is filled with little jokes and puns as well as plenty of math.

Point out to students that this is an interesting multiplication rule: No matter what number you multiply by 0—even if it's huge, like 1,000,000—you will still get 0.

On the transparency, highlight those sections of machines that had 1 card stuck. Ask: "What do these sections have in common?" (*One card was stuck in each machine.*) "Was there anything you noticed about figuring the card totals for these sections?" (*If you multiply a number by 1, you get the original number.*)

Explain to students that these interesting patterns can help us memorize multiplication facts. Hold up a copy of the 100 Multiplication Facts Chart and point out that of the 100 multiplication facts on the chart, 36 of those facts use 0s or 1s. More than one-third of the whole chart! Write these facts on the board or show on the overhead.

$0 \times 0 = 0$	$1 \times 0 = 0$	$1 \times 1 = 1$	$2 \times 1 = 2$
$0 \times 1 = 0$	$2 \times 0 = 0$	$1 \times 2 = 2$	$3 \times 1 = 3$
$0 \times 2 = 0$	$3 \times 0 = 0$	$1 \times 3 = 3$	$4 \times 1 = 4$
$0 \times 3 = 0$	$4 \times 0 = 0$	$1 \times 4 = 4$	$5 \times 1 = 5$
$0 \times 4 = 0$	$5 \times 0 = 0$	$1 \times 5 = 5$	$6 \times 1 = 6$
$0 \times 5 = 0$	$6 \times 0 = 0$	$1 \times 6 = 6$	$7 \times 1 = 7$
$0 \times 6 = 0$	$7 \times 0 = 0$	$1 \times 7 = 7$	$8 \times 1 = 8$
$0 \times 7 = 0$	$8 \times 0 = 0$	$1 \times 8 = 8$	$9 \times 1 = 9$
$0 \times 8 = 0$	$9 \times 0 = 0$	$1 \times 9 = 9$	
$0 \times 9 = 0$			

Invite students to fill in a Math Secrets page and 100 Multiplication Facts Chart for each of these ideas. Pass out two copies of each page to each student. These can be completed in class or for homework.

ACTIVITY: How Low Can You Go? Dice Game
(2 to 4 players)

Blank dice are readily available at many school supply stores and catalogs. They usually come with blank round stickers on which you can write numbers or spots of your choosing. Prepare a pair of dice. On one die write the numbers 1 to 6. On another, write three 0s and three 1s. To play, have students roll the dice, multiply the two numbers that come up, and write the product. Each player gets five rolls. Players record the product for each roll. The lowest total wins. This gives students some fun practice multiplying by zeros and ones.

ACTIVITY LESSON #6

Forest Baseball Cards

(Nifty Nines Strategy for Multiplication)

Overview: Students will learn several strategies for understanding and memorization of nines facts.

Tell the class, "We have a new letter from Mr. Cardenza, and it is a bit unusual." Pass out copies of Letter #6 to students. Allow students to read silently, then read the letter aloud together.

Put a transparency of the letter on the overhead. Ask: "What do all the baseball teams in his letter have in common?" (*They are all in the forest, and they all have 9 players on a team.*) Have students work with a partner to fill in the order form. When they are done, call on volunteers to fill in the answers on the chart on the overhead. Ask the class: "What kind of multiplication facts are helpful here?" (*Nines facts*)

Invite students to share any good strategies they might have for helping them remember nines facts. Discuss their strategies and summarize them on the board. Explain to students that sometimes you can find strategies by looking for patterns in the factors and products. List the nines facts on the board and have students copy them on a piece of paper.

9 × 0 = 0	9 × 5 = 45
9 × 1 = 9	9 × 6 = 54
9 × 2 = 18	9 × 7 = 63
9 × 3 = 27	9 × 8 = 72
9 × 4 = 36	9 × 9 = 81

Have students work with a partner to look for any patterns in these facts. Give students up to ten minutes and then have them report back about patterns they see.

Discuss the Nifty Nines strategy with students: "Notice that if we add the digits of the product, they always add up to 9. Take for example 9 × 7 = 63. In this case, 6 + 3 = 9. Notice also that the first digit of the product is always 1 less than the second factor. So the 6 in 63 is 1 less than the factor 7. If we were to look just at the expression 9 × 7, we could say, well, 1 less than 7 is 6. I know 6 is the first digit of the product. I also know the two digits in the product must add up to 9, so that would be 6 + 3 or 63!" This is easier to diagram on the board than it is to explain.

Materials

For each student:
- Letter #6 (p. 54)
- Math Secret (p. 43)
- 100 Multiplication Facts Chart (p. 44)
- Practice Page #6 (p. 55)
- Review Page #6 (p. 56)
- pencil

For teacher:
- Transparency of Letter #6
- overhead markers

Teaching Tip

Beginning with a Question or Problem

A simple but very powerful teaching strategy is to begin every math lesson with a problem or question that embodies the concept or skill you are teaching in that lesson. This provides a reason and context for the ideas you want students to learn. Even if you are required to use a textbook lesson, you can still read over the lesson and decide what a good opening word problem or question might be that would require the skill or concept you are going to study. This creates a spirit of inquiry in class and shows that everything you teach has an application and a purpose—to help solve real-life problems.

9 × 7

One less than 7 is 6.

6 must be the first digit of the product ——▶ 6____

6 + ____ = 9

6 + 3 = 9, so 3 is the second digit of the product <u>63</u>

Repeat this strategy with a few more nines facts with your students. Then have them fill in a Math Secret page and the 100 Multiplication Facts Chart for the Nifty Nines strategy.

. . . .

Materials

For each student:

• Letter #7 (p. 57)

• Double-Doubler Machines (p. 58)

• Math Secret (p. 43)

• 100 Multiplication Facts Chart (p. 44)

• Practice Page #7 (p. 59)

• Review Page #7 (p. 60)

• pencil

Teaching Tip

Multiplication Practice Online

If you have the Internet available in your class, you might want to check out http://www.scholastic. com. The site offers many interactive math games for free use. Students can practice their multiplication facts independently in a fun and safe Web environment.

ACTIVITY LESSON #7

On the Double-Double!

(DOUBLING STRATEGY WITH FOURS FACTS)

> **Overview:** Students will learn to extend their doubling skills to calculate multiples of 4.

Tell the class: "I had a feeling we would hear from Mr. Cardenza today, and here he is!" Pass out copies of Letter #7 to students. Have everyone read it silently, then read the letter aloud.

Review the Doubles strategy for finding the twos facts. Then explain to students that to find products for the fours facts, we're going to double the factors twice. For example, to find the answer to 4 × 8, first double 8 to get 16. Then double 16 to get 32.

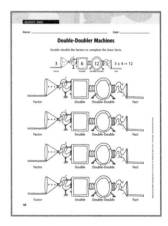

Give each student a copy of the Double-Doubler Machines page. Tell students to work with a math partner to complete the fours facts on the Double-Doubler Machines. They'll need to double the factors and then double them again to show how the machines will work.

Review the first example on the paper together and do these next two on the board:

8 × 4 = ?   Double 8 = 16

Double that answer = 32

$$4 \times 4 = ? \qquad \text{Double } 4 = 8$$
$$\text{Double that answer} = 16$$

When students have completed their sheets, review their work together. Ask students: "Which fours facts are the toughest? Does anyone have any helping strategies for the tougher doubles?" At the conclusion of the lesson have students complete a Math Secret sheet and a 100 Multiplication Facts Chart for the Double-Double strategy.

ACTIVITY: **Multiplication Brain Game**

This is an exciting game that can be used to practice multiplication facts and the concept of a missing factor. Take an ordinary deck of playing cards and remove all jokers, kings, queens, jacks, and tens. Shuffle the deck and place it facedown between two players in the front of the class. Each player draws a card without looking and places it on his or her "brain" (forehead) with the card facing the rest of the class. On your signal, the class shouts out the product of the two cards. The players turn and face each other so they can see each other's cards. Now each player knows the product and the other factor. The first to call out his own factor (the missing factor) wins. You can focus this practice on certain groups of facts by removing cards from the deck or make it more challenging by putting two decks together.

Teaching Tip

Big Paper for Big Ideas

Large pieces of roll paper can be a useful math teaching tool. The big workspace allows students to show their math ideas with pictures and diagrams and more. Give a small group of students a big piece of paper and ask them to show how to solve a multiplication problem or set of facts using pictures, numbers, and words. Or ask students to show how to solve a single multiplication problem as many different ways as they can. When students have more than the usual 8½-by-11-inch sheet of paper and a little extra time, they can explore new math ideas in more depth and detail.

ACTIVITY LESSON #8

Lawn Chairs of Antarctica 3-Coin Sets

(DOUBLE-PLUS-ONE STRATEGY FOR THREES FACTS)

Overview: Students will use doubling factors and adding single sets to compute multiples of 3.

Tell students: "Mr. Cardenza is back, and it looks like we might have some more doubling to do." Distribute copies of Letter #8 to students and have them read it silently. Read the letter aloud and discuss the problem. Ask students: "What do you remember about doubling? How do you think doubling could help us with threes facts?" Discuss.

Materials

For each student:

- Letter #8 (p. 61)
- Math Secret (p. 43)
- 100 Multiplication Facts Chart (p. 44)
- set of 30 pennies or counters for each partner group (optional)
- Practice Page #8 (p. 62)
- Review Page #8 (p. 63)
- pencil

Teaching Tip

Student Creativity for Facts Strategies

Throughout this book you will find strategies that many mathematicians and math educators have developed to help students learn and memorize multiplication facts. However, sometimes students come up with some great, unique strategies of their own. During these lessons on strategies, try to allow some time for students to share strategies that they may be using themselves to solve multiplication problems. Sometimes ideas from classmates resonate more with peers than ideas from other sources.

Materials

For each student:
- Letter #9 (p. 64)
- Math Secret (p. 43)
- 100 Multiplication Facts Chart (p. 44)
- Practice Page #9 (p. 65)
- Review Page #9 (p. 66)
- pencil

$3 \times 8 = ?$

$$\begin{array}{r} 16 \\ + 8 \\ \hline 24 \end{array}$$

Explain how this new Double-Plus-One strategy works: To find products for threes facts, first double the factor you're multiplying by 3, and then add one more group of that factor. Take for example 3×8. First, double 8 to get 16. Now, add one more group of 8 to 16—that would be 24. So, $3 \times 8 = 24$. Invite students to share other examples to include on their Math Secret page.

Have students work with a partner to help Mr. Cardenza with his 3-coin packs project. If desired, give each partner group 30 pennies or counters to model this strategy or use as manipulatives as they work. Review partner work as a class. Share any student strategies for solving tougher facts. At the conclusion of the lesson have students complete the Math Secret sheet and a 100 Multiplication Fact Chart for the Double-Plus-One strategy.

ACTIVITY: Two Sets and an Extra: Practicing Threes Facts

Cut photographs from magazines and create sets of items (e.g., 7 dwarves, 6 packs of soda, 9 ballplayers, etc.). Glue two sets of the item on a piece of paper and then add one more set. Label your sets with a number sentence to teach the related threes fact: 2 sets of 6 soda cans is 12 soda cans, plus 1 more set of 6 is 18. So 3×6 is 18. If you can't find enough pictures, have students draw them or use rubber stamps as needed.

ACTIVITY LESSON #9

A Tough Order

(FRIENDLY CHUNKS STRATEGY FOR SIXES, SEVENS, AND EIGHTS FACTS)

Overview: The next two activity lessons focus on "helper" strategies that can assist students in learning the often more difficult facts found in the sixes, sevens, and eights times tables.

Tell the class, "You mathematicians are getting so good at your multiplication facts that now you're ready for toughest of the tough. Let's see what Mr. Cardenza has to say about the trickiest facts." Pass out copies of Letter #9 and let students read silently before reading it aloud together.

Say, "Let's take a look at this Friendly Chunks idea. This strategy will work on almost any fact. Let's try it on 8 × 7. We can make 8 groups of 7 into two easier fact problems or "chunks." We can begin with 3 × 7, or 3 groups of 7, and 5 × 7, or 5 groups of 7. Those are easier facts, aren't they? We know that 3 groups of 7 is 21. And we know our fives facts pretty well, so we know that 5 groups of 7 is 35. Let's add those products together: 21 + 35. Well, 35 + 20 = 55, plus 1 more is 56. So the answer to 8 × 7 is 56." Diagram this on the board as you explain.

$$8 \times 7 = (3 \times 7) + (5 \times 7)$$
$$8 \times 7 = 21 + 35$$
$$8 \times 7 = 56$$

Ask students: "Why do you think this strategy is called Friendly Chunks?" (*The problem is split into smaller chunks, each of which is easier to solve than the larger problem by itself.*)

Try the Friendly Chunks strategy with another "tough" problem, like 9 × 8. Ask students how they could break up 9 groups of 8. (*Some possible solutions include: 4 × 8 plus 5 × 8, or 3 × 8 = 24, plus another 24 [48] plus another 24 [72]*) Write these solutions on the board. If necessary, model one or two other facts for students.

Tell students to try using the Friendly Chunks strategy to complete the order form in Mr. Cardenza's letter. Have them work with a partner and write down the Friendly Chunks they used to solve each problem. After students have finished, review and discuss together.

At the conclusion of the lesson have students complete a Math Secret sheet and a 100 Multiplication Facts Chart for the Friendly Chunks strategy. Since this strategy can be used for many facts, have students highlight eight facts on the 100 Multiplication Facts Chart where this strategy might be applied.

ACTIVITY: Friendly Chunk Arrays

Provide students with simple stickers such as color dots or stars. Have students use the stickers to make arrays for tricky facts (like 7 × 8) on construction paper. Then have them use scissors to cut the arrays into Friendly Chunks—7 groups of 8 becomes 5 groups of 8 and 2 more groups of 8. Glue the new Friendly Chunks next to each other on larger pieces of paper and have students label the chunks with the chunk facts and products. Then write the addition problem that will give them the answer to the tough fact (in this example, 40 + 16 = 56, so 7 × 8 = 56).

Teaching Tip

My Favorite Helper Facts

Have students illustrate their most useful "helper fact" and explain which additional problems the helper fact could help them to solve. For example, 7 x 7 = 49 is a good helper fact because it can help us remember 7 x 8 = 56. This is a good project for a bulletin board display.

Literature Link

Sea Squares by Joy Hulme (Hyperion, 1991)

Beautiful illustrations of sea life with embedded multiplication and a smooth rhyming text make this a favorite picture book. Focusing primarily on squares (1 x 1, 2 x 2, 3 x 3, . . .), it is deeper than it first appears. Have students check out the clever way the author creates groups and uses her border illustrations to foreshadow what comes next.

Activity: **Tell-Me-the-Strategy Deck**

Take a deck of multiplication flash cards. Flash a card to the class and ask for a strategy for solving it, then the answer. This may seem to slow the process down—and it does temporarily—but in the long run it helps students internalize strong number-sense strategies that they can fall back on if the fact is not readily available to them. Another variation on this is to arrange the set of cards so only certain strategies are shown, such as all the 0 and 1 cards. In this way a strategy can be focused on and practiced with regular multiplication flash cards.

ACTIVITY LESSON #10

A Tough Order, Part 2

(HALF-THEN-DOUBLE STRATEGY FOR SIXES, SEVENS, AND EIGHTS FACTS)

> **Overview:** Students will learn the Half-Then-Double strategy for use with sixes, sevens, and eights facts.

Materials

For each student:

• Letter #10 (p. 67)

• Math Secret (p. 43)

• 100 Multiplication Facts Chart (p. 44)

• Practice Page #10 (p. 69)

• Review Page #10 (p. 70)

• pencil

Review the Friendly Chunks strategy with the class and how it helps with tougher facts. Tell students, "Sounds like we're ready to move on to the next advanced Math Secret strategy. Let's see what Mr. Cardenza has to say about what we need to do today." Pass out copies of Letter #10 to students. Let them read the letter silently, then read it aloud together.

Explain to students that the Half-Then-Double strategy works with any fact that has at least one even factor, such as 4×7 or 6×8. Ask: "Will it work on 5×7? Why?" (No, because both factors are odd.)

Try out the strategy with a fact problem that has at least one even factor, like 6×7. Draw 6 sets of 7 objects on the board or overhead projector as you explain: "We need to figure out how many is 6 groups of 7. What's half of 6?" (3) "So we know that 3 groups of 7 is 21—that's an easier fact. Then all I have to do is double that product: $21 + 21 = 42$. So 6 groups of 7 is 42."

$6 \times 7 = ?$

$3 \times 7 = 21$

$3 \times 7 = 21$

$21 + 21 = 42$

$6 \times 7 = 42$

On another part of the board, begin another example, making sure to leave room for diagrams. Say: "Let's try one more. We'll use 4×9. Let's take half of the even factor—that'll be 2. What is 2 groups of 9?" *(18)* "And $18 + 18$ is 36. So, 4×9 is 36."

Invite students to work with a partner on Mr. Cardenza's order form in the letter. Have them use the Half-Then-Double strategy wherever it makes sense and fill in the chart to show their thinking. Allow students time to complete the chart then review answers and strategies together.

At the conclusion of the lesson have students complete a Math Secret sheet and a 100 Multiplication Facts Chart for the Half-Then-Double strategy. With so many facts on the chart that could use this strategy, have students pick out and highlight eight examples.

ACTIVITY: **Where Does It Work?**

This activity can be used to practice any multiplication strategy. List a set of problems and simply ask: "Which of these can be solved using the target strategy?" In other words, where does the strategy work? For example, with the Half-Then-Double strategy, you might want to use something like this:

> **Which of these card, coin, and shoe orders can be solved using the Half-Then-Double method?**
>
> **1.** 4 sets of 3 coins
>
> **2.** 8 sets of 6 shoes
>
> **3.** 3 packs of 5 cards
>
> **4.** 6 packs of 9 shoes

Students should be able to explain where it works and why, as well as where it would not work and why. This helps students think conceptually about the strategies and helps them develop a strong foundation of understanding about what they are doing when they multiply.

Teaching Tip

Almost Facts or Related Facts

Almost Facts or Related Facts is a strategy that can be used on many different facts. The idea is to look at a given fact and see if there are any similar facts that you readily know the answer to that you can use to solve the more difficult fact. For example, if 6×7 is difficult, we can think $7 \times 7 = 49$, so if I take one less 7, that's 42. Another example might be 9×6. We know tens facts are easy so $10 \times 6 = 60$. 6 less than 60 is 54.

The idea to impress upon students is that if a fact does not come immediately to mind, they can consider the fact that is before or after it in sequence to see if that fact is easier and thus can become a helper. To practice this strategy, have students complete the Almost-a-Sport Card Order Form on page 68. Tell the class that this is an order form for cards for activities that are classified as "almost sports," such as Ping-Pong Ball Hockey or Beachball Baseball. For fun, have students make up their own "almost sports" and include the names of these sports as part of the order.

Materials

For each student:

- Letter #11 (p. 71)
- Math Secrets (p. 43)
- 100 Multiplication Facts Chart (p. 44)
- Practice Page #11 (p. 72)
- Review Page #11 (p. 73)
- pencil

For teachers:

- Transparency of Letter #11
- overhead markers

Literature Link

The Best of Times: Math Strategies That Multiply by Greg Tang (Scholastic, 2002)

Clever poems and fun illustrations help reinforce many useful multiplication strategies in this colorful, large-format picture book. The individual poems would make a great introduction to the strategies we've presented here. The back of Tang's book includes a reference section that summarizes the strategies and includes a list of facts appropriate to each strategy. This is a really excellent and motivating resource for any classroom.

ACTIVITY LESSON #11

Packing Coin Sets

(*Commutative Property of Multiplication*)

> **Overview:** Students learn that multiplication is commutative—even when factors are reversed, they still yield the same product.

Announce to the class: "We have a new letter from Mr. Cardenza. In fact, this one talks about a new product." Give each student a copy of Letter #11 to read silently. Then read the letter aloud.

Have students work with a partner to fill in the order form. When students are finished, put a transparency of the letter on the overhead and discuss.

Ask: "What do you notice about organizing these coin sets? What do they all have in common?" (*Even when reversed, the factors yield the same product.*) Tell students that this is another interesting fact about multiplication. It is called the *commutative property*.

Draw 2 circles on the board and put 5 stars in each circle. Say, "Here we have 10 stars. There are 5 in one circle and 5 in the other. How could I represent this with a multiplication fact?" ($2 \times 5 = 10$) "Now, what if I draw this a different way?" Draw 5 circles and put 2 stars in each. "I still have 10 stars, but now they are arranged differently. What multiplication fact could describe this?" ($5 \times 2 = 10$) Explain to students that this is the commutative property of multiplication: We can reverse the factors and still get the same product. The order doesn't matter.

Tell students that this idea is helpful because they are always free to reverse the factors if it will help them solve the fact. For example, say you have the fact 7×9. Maybe you are not that comfortable with your sevens facts, but you know your nines facts and the Nifty Nines strategy. All you have to do is reverse the factors so it reads 9×7. Now you can use your strategy and the product will be the same. Tell students that if they come across a fact that they find hard to remember, try reversing the factors to see if that gives them a better handle on it.

Ask for volunteers to share more examples on the board. Then have students complete a Math Secret sheet for the Commutative Property of Multiplication. Note that this is the last Math Secret. Students can now keep the Math Secrets Handbook as a handy reference. On the 100 Multiplication Facts Chart, have students highlight five pairs of facts that demonstrate the commutative property.

ACTIVITY: **Commutative Card Game Match**
(2 players)

Take a deck of multiplication flash cards and put them facedown between two players. Players take turns picking a card from the deck. If a player can say the product of the fact within five seconds, she can keep the card. The object of the game is to get two fact cards that show the commutative property. For example, say a player picks a 5 × 7 card, correctly answers 35, and gets to keep the card. If the player later picks a 7 × 5 card and answers correctly again, he scores a point. When all the cards have been drawn, each player totals the number of commutative card pairs he or she has. The player with the most points wins.

ACTIVITY LESSON #12

Best Umbrellas of the 20th Century
(MULTIPLICATION PATTERNS)

Overview: Students will learn how patterns in multiplication by 1s, 10s, and 100s can be helpful in more complex multiplication equations.

Tell the class, "Would you believe, another letter from Mr. Cardenza?" Pass out a copy of Letter #12 to each student. Have everyone read it silently, then read it aloud.

Have students work with a partner to fill in the Famous Umbrellas Order form. When students are finished, review their answers together on the board or overhead. The answers will look like this:

$$3 \times 1 = 3$$
$$3 \times 10 = 30$$
$$3 \times 100 = 300$$

$$6 \times 1 = 6$$
$$6 \times 10 = 60$$
$$6 \times 100 = 600$$

Ask the class: "Do you notice any patterns here that might be helpful to Mr. Cardenza and save him the trouble of using a calculator?" Discuss ideas and summarize. Explain that place value patterns can help us multiply by 10s, 100s, or even 1,000s.

Materials

For each student:
- Letter #12 (p. 74)
- Practice Page #12 (p. 75)
- Review Page #12 (p. 76)
- pencil

Teaching Tip

Visualize and Strategize

Sometimes students who struggle with memorization of multiplication facts by rote respond well to visual representations, which they can internalize and call up as needed. To help support this learning style, draw facts in arrays on graph paper or use sticky dots to create sets of facts that have a visual organization. This can make a great bulletin board with all 100 facts displayed with accompanying pictorial arrays.

For example, when we multiply by 10s (as in 60 × 3), we can begin by writing a 0 in the tens place, then multiply the remaining non-zero digits.

$$
\begin{array}{r} 60 \\ \times\ 3 \\ \hline 0 \end{array}
\qquad
\begin{array}{r} 60 \\ \times\ 3 \\ \hline 180 \end{array}
$$

To check, or even to begin, count the 0s in the factors. That's how many 0s you should have in the product.

To multiply by 100s, write two 0s in the product, one in the ones place and one in the tens place. Then multiply the non-zero digits.

$$
\begin{array}{r} 700 \\ \times\ 5 \\ \hline 00 \end{array}
\qquad
\begin{array}{r} 700 \\ \times\ 5 \\ \hline 3500 \end{array}
$$

Once again, we can check that there are two 0s in the factors and then two 0s in the product. This can also help us decide if the answer is reasonable.

For practice, assign each partner group a single-digit number from 1 to 9. Have them multiply the number by 1, 10, and 100, and then share their results with the class. For a bigger challenge, assign each pair double-digit numbers to multiply by 1, 10, and 100.

ACTIVITY: **Multiplication Calculator Patterns**

To continue reviewing basic facts, partner up students and give them a calculator to share. Assign each partner group a times table to review. The first partner will then "program" the calculator with that times table. For example, if you assign the threes facts, the lead partner presses 3 and then +. Then, by pressing =, the product of the number of presses times the number on the button pressed (in this case, 3) will come up on the screen. Partners can run straight through the times table or try out random facts from the table on each other. This activity makes fact review a little more unique and provides students with some hands-on calculator experience.

ACTIVITY LESSON #13

Amazing Collector Coins

(METHODS OF MULTIPLICATION: SINGLE- BY DOUBLE-DIGIT MULTIPLICATION)

> Overview: Students will learn two methods of multiplying double-digit by single-digit numbers—the traditional method and using partial products.

Materials

For each student:
- Letter #13 (p. 77)
- Practice Page #13 (p. 78)
- Review Page #13 (p. 79)
- pencil

Tell students that another letter from Mr. Cardenza has arrived. Distribute copies of the letter and have students read it silently before reading it together aloud.

Say, "Let's take a look at that first order. They have to make 17 sets of Furniture Coins. How do we calculate this?" *(A set of Furniture Coins has 6 coins in it, so we would have to add 17 six times, or multiply 17 × 6)*

Set up the problem 17 × 6 on the board or overhead.

$$\begin{array}{r} 17 \\ \times\ 6 \\ \hline \end{array}$$

Tell students, "I'm going to demonstrate two methods of multiplying these numbers. In this first method, I multiply the numbers in the ones place first, so 7 × 6 = 42.

"I write it like this, and since 42 has 4 tens and 2 ones, I leave the 2 in the ones place and regroup the 4 tens above the tens place.

$$\begin{array}{r} 4\ \ \ \\ 17 \\ \times\ 6 \\ \hline 2 \end{array}$$

27

Teaching Tip

....

Labeling for Meaning

When students are solving word problems or problems from a context such as those found in Mr. Cardenza's letters, get them in the habit of using labels for their answers. Labeling the products, and even the factors, is a good way to help students keep track of what they are doing and make sure their manipulations of the numbers are meaningful and make sense. This is especially important when the labels involve measurements and money units.

Now I multiply again, this time I multiply the 6 in the ones place by the 10 in the tens place. This would be 60. There are the 4 tens I regrouped before, which are also in the tens. I need to add these 4 tens to the 6 tens to get 10 tens. I put the 10 in the tens part of the product to show 100. The ones place shows 2, so the product is 102.

$$
\begin{array}{r}
4 \\
1\,7 \\
\times\ 6 \\
\hline
6\ +\ 4 \longrightarrow 1\,0\,2
\end{array}
$$

Have students work with a partner to work on the second order using this traditional method. When students have completed this, share the solution and method on the board. Then have students work in pairs again to work on the third order of 25 sets of Ice Cream Coins, still using the same method as the previous two problems.

After reviewing the answer together, say, "Now, let's look at another method we could use to multiply. This method is called Partial Products." Set up the Ice Cream Coin problem (25 × 9) on the board.

Explain that with Partial Products we split the number open a bit: "First, we look at the ones, as before, and multiply 5 × 9 to get 45. This time, however, we don't regroup anything. We just leave the 45 to the side.

$$
\begin{array}{r}
2\,5 \\
\times\ 9 \\
\hline
 = 4\,5
\end{array}
$$

"Now we look at the rest of the equation. We see 20 and 9. We multiply these two factors to get 180. We know 2 × 9 = 18, and multiplication patterns tell us if there is a 0 in the factors, there should be the same number of 0s in the product.

$$\begin{array}{r} 25 \\ \times\ 9 \\ \hline \end{array} = 180$$

"So we have two 'partial' products: 180 and 45. All we have to do now is add them to get the total product of 225."

$$\begin{array}{r} 180 \\ +\ \ 45 \\ \hline 225 \end{array}$$

Explain that Partial Products is a good strategy for multiplying two-digit numbers if you prefer doing the two smaller multiplications without regrouping. If you prefer regrouping rather than breaking the number open and doing the addition, stick with the first method. A good strategy to check your work is to simply do the other method. Have students go back and complete the first two problems using the Partial Products method.

Literature Link

....

Anno's Mysterious Multiplying Jar by Masaichiro and Mitsumasa Anno (Philomel, 1983)

High-level multiplication in a deceptively simple story with elegant illustrations can be used in a simple way or as an entry to some very challenging multiplication ideas, including exponents. Students will enjoy puzzling out the numbers in this one.

Part 2: Division

Materials

For each student:

- Letter #14 (p. 80)
- Practice Page #14 (p. 82)
- Review Page #14 (p. 83)
- pencil

Teaching Tip

Checking Division with Multiplication

From the very beginning of working with division, have students check their work by doing the corresponding multiplication. This will help students check answers in an efficient way and will also help build operational number sense as they see the strong relationship between the two operations.

Literature Link

The Great Divide
by Dayle Ann Dodds
(Candlewick Press, 1999)

A large group of people in a cross-country race is continually divided in 2 by circumstances along the way. The race finally narrows down to one winner. (You might be surprised by who it is.) This is a good book for beginning a discussion of basic division patterns.

ACTIVITY LESSON #14

Leftover Coins

(INTRODUCING DIVISION: ONE-DIGIT DIVISORS WITHOUT REMAINDERS)

> **Overview:** Students will explore dividing with one-digit divisors and no remainders.

Announce to students: "We have another challenging request from Mr. Cardenza." Pass out copies of Letter #14 to students. Have them read the letter silently, then read it aloud together. Say, "This is interesting. This set of orders is a little different. How is it different from the previous orders?" (*Multiplication will not solve these problems, but division will. Knowing multiplication facts will help, however.*)

Engage students in a discussion about division and what it is. Focus on the idea that division is an operation that shares or divides a number or number of objects into equal groups or fair shares. Explain that division is the inverse, or opposite, of multiplication.

Say, "Let's look at the first order. There are 25 coins that Mr. Cardenza wants to put into medium-size sets. A medium-size set has 5 coins in it. How do we know how many sets that will make?" (*Divide 25 by 5*) "We want to put 5 coins in each set, so that means we can make 5 sets of 5 coins in each. Knowing the multiplication fact $5 \times 5 = 25$ helps us figure out the division." Draw this division of the coins on the board.

Explain that there are two ways to write this division problem. Draw both algorithms and label the parts: *divisor, dividend,* and *quotient.*

$$25 \div 5 = 5$$

dividend   divisor   quotient

$$\text{quotient} \quad 5$$
$$5\overline{)25}$$

divisor   dividend

Have students work with a partner or individually to complete the order form in Mr. Cardenza's letter. Make sure students write the multiplication fact they used to help them. When they're finished, review their answers and methods together.

Activity: **Find-the-Multiplication-Card Game**

(2 to 4 players)

Photocopy a set of the multiplication and division cards on page 81. Laminate them and cut the cards apart. Shuffle the cards, then spread them on a desk facedown. Players take turns picking two cards at a time. If a player gets a division card and a corresponding multiplication card (e.g., 10 ÷ 5 and 5 × 2), he keeps the pair. The player with the most matching pairs at the end of the game wins.

ACTIVITY LESSON #15

Sharing the Sock Cards

(ONE-DIGIT DIVISORS WITH REMAINDERS)

> Overview: Students will learn about division with single-digit divisors and remainders.

Tell students that another letter from Mr. Cardenza has arrived. Pass out copies of Letter #15 and provide time for students to read silently. Then read the letter aloud together.

Copy the Printing Press A data from the letter onto the board and ask students: "How did Mr. Cardenza figure out the number of cards for each worker for this machine?" (*He divided the number of cards by the number of workers: 25 ÷ 5 = 5 cards for each worker*)

Say, "Let's try the same thing for Press B. In fact, let's draw what it would look like." Draw 30 small rectangles on the board to represent cards, then draw 5 stick figures underneath to represent people.

Materials

For each student:

- Letter #15 (p. 84)
- Practice Page #15 (p. 86)
- Review Page #15 (p. 87)
- pencil

Teaching Tip

Index Card Blocker

The long-division algorithm can be hard to follow and keep organized. For students who have difficulty keeping things in line, consider providing them with a simple blank index card. Students can use the card to cover up sections of the problem so that it is easier to focus on one section at a time. As students complete the problem, they slide the card to the right, revealing each new section to be dealt with.

Step-by-Step Bring-Down Method of Division

$$7\overline{)127}$$

7 doesn't go into 1, so move on to the tens. 7 goes into 12 one time.

$$\begin{array}{r} 1 \\ 7\overline{)127} \\ \underline{7} \end{array}$$

Multiply 1 by 7 to get 7, then subtract from 12.

$$\begin{array}{r} 1 \\ 7\overline{)127} \\ \underline{7} \\ 5 \end{array}$$

Bring down the 7 from 127.

$$\begin{array}{r} 18 \\ 7\overline{)127} \\ \underline{7}\downarrow \\ 57 \end{array}$$

Multiply 8 by 7 to get 56, then subtract from 57.

$$\begin{array}{r} 18\,r1 \\ 7\overline{)127} \\ \underline{7} \\ 57 \\ \underline{56} \\ 1 \end{array}$$

1 is the remainder.

Call on a volunteer to show how to divide the cards up evenly. (*The student should circle 5 groups of cards and connect each group to a person. There should be 6 cards for each worker.*) Ask students: "What multiplication fact describes this?" (*6 × 5 = 30*) Remind students that multiplication facts can help us with division or fair sharing.

Continue: "Next let's try Press C. We still have 30 cards, but now we are sharing with 4 people. Will they get more or less cards this time?" (*More cards, because there are fewer people sharing the same amount*) "So do you think they can get 7 cards each?" (*Yes, because 7 × 4 = 28*) "Does that work out evenly?" (*No, there are 2 extra cards*)

Explain that when we divide, sometimes the result comes out with perfectly equal fair shares. But sometimes, as in this case, there are leftovers, which are called *remainders*. Show how this is written.

$$\begin{array}{r} 7\,r2 \\ 4\overline{)30} \\ \underline{28} \\ 2 \end{array}$$

Have students work with a partner to try Press D and E. Review their answers as above. Draw diagrams on the board as necessary to show fair shares and remainders.

Tell students: "Let's look at Press F. That has 100 cards, and they have to be shared among 6 people. Could each person get 20 cards?" (*No, because you would need 120 cards*) "Could each person get 19 cards?" (*No, because then you'd need 114 cards*) Explain that we are trying to start with an estimate of about how many cards each person could get and then trying to see if that estimate works. We want to get as close to the target number as we can before trying division. Have students try this strategy with their partner to come up with the answer. Then invite them to share their ideas and work on the board.

Continue: "So, if we try 18, that would be 100 ÷ 18 or 18 × 6, which is what?" (*108*) "We're close here. What should we try next?" (*17*) "Oh, 102—that is so close! What next?" (*16*) 16 × 6 = 96. Ask students: "Why is 96 okay?" (*It is as close to 100 as we can get without going over. Then each worker gets 16 cards and we have a reminder of 4.*) Write the equation on the board, making sure to highlight the remainder.

Have students work with partners to fill in the rest of the order form. Circulate and help students as needed. When they're finished, invite students to share and discuss their answers.

Use Press H to show the step-by-step Bring-Down method for dividing a three-digit number by a one-digit number with regrouping (see left).

ACTIVITY: **I-Want-Remainders Game**
(2 to 4 players)

Make copies of the "I Want Remainders" number cards and spinner (p. 85). Shuffle the cards and stack them. To play, pick a number card from the deck. This is the number you must divide. Using a pencil and paper clip for a spinning device, spin the spinner. This is the number you will divide by. If a player can divide the number on the card by the number on the spinner evenly (with no remainder), the card goes in the discard pile. If there is a remainder and the player states it correctly, he gets to keep the card. Each card kept is worth one point. The player with the most cards (points) at the end of the game wins.

ACTIVITY LESSON #16

Favorite Fruit Commemorative Coins

(TWO-DIGIT DIVISORS)

> Overview: Students will learn how to divide by double-digit divisors using the Bring-Down method.

Announce to the class: "Another letter from Mr. Cardenza, and he's having trouble selling some special coins." Pass out copies of Letter #16 to students. Have them read the letter silently, then read it aloud together.

Ask students: "How will we figure out how many coins to give each player and how many will be left over?" (*Divide the number of coins by the number of players*) Have students work with a partner to figure out the first order. When they're finished, invite them to share their answer and the method they used.

Write the information about the Ocelots order on the board: 124 ÷ 11.

Tell students, "We're going to use the Bring-Down method like we did last lesson and look carefully to see if it still works with bigger numbers in the divisor and in the dividend." Ask students to help with each step of the Bring-Down method as you solve the problem on the board (see right).

Literature Link

A Remainder of One
by Elinor J. Pinczes
(Houghton Mifflin, 1995)

The 15th Insect Squadron marches in parade formation. Soldier Joe has trouble fitting in. It seems he is always the remainder. As formations change, so do the multiplication arrays and division problems possible to describe these illustrations. Joe finally gets to join the formation when there are 25 soldiers in 5 lines of 5. You can have students write the division equations to match the various formations of ants in the pictures.

Materials

For each student:
- Letter #16 (p. 88)
- Practice Page #16 (p. 90)
- Review Page #16 (p. 91)
- pencil

$$11\overline{)124} \quad 1$$
$$11$$
$$1$$

$$11\overline{)124} \quad 11$$
$$11$$
$$14$$
$$11$$
$$3$$

$$11\overline{)124} \quad 1$$
$$11$$
$$14$$

$$11\overline{)124} \quad 11\ r3$$
$$11$$
$$14$$
$$11$$
$$3$$

Teaching Tip

. . . .

Thank-You Letter

To help close the unit, make a copy of the Thank-You Letter (p. 92) and The Most Valuable Mathematician Card (p. 93) for each student. This is a good-bye and thank-you letter from Mr. Cardenza, plus a little surprise fun piece of artwork that students will enjoy as they draw their self-portraits on the Most Valuable Mathematician Card template.

Demonstrate this one more time with the next order in Mr. Cardenza's letter. Then challenge students to fill in the rest of the order with a partner or on their own. Review their answers together.

ACTIVITY: **Causing Problems Game** (2 to 4 players)

Make copies of the number cards and the game board on page 89. Players take turns picking a number card from the deck. As a player picks a card, she may place it on a space on the game board, put it off to one side, or exchange it for another card. She can also move cards already on the game board at any time. The first player to create a division problem with dividend, divisor, quotient, and if needed, remainder, wins. Have the player record her equation. Return the used cards to the deck and shuffle the deck before starting another round.

Teaching Tip

. . . .

Dividing with 0s in the Quotient

Sometimes a 0 in the quotient can cause some confusion for students. For example, say we are dividing $630 \div 6$. Dividing the hundreds is easy because $6 \div 6 = 1$.

$$\begin{array}{r} 1 \\ 6\overline{)630} \\ \underline{6} \\ 0 \end{array}$$

Next, we bring down the 3. Since we can't divide 6 into 3, we need to show that in the quotient by placing a 0.

$$\begin{array}{r} 10 \\ 6\overline{)630} \\ \underline{6}\downarrow \\ 03 \end{array}$$

Finally, we bring down the 0. We now have 30, which we can divide evenly by 6. Add 5 to the quotient ($5 \times 6 = 30$) to get 105.

$$\begin{array}{r} 105 \\ 6\overline{)630} \\ \underline{6} \\ \underline{03}\downarrow \\ 30 \end{array}$$

Two tips to help students with this process:

First, have students estimate an answer. In this case, we can see the answer will be about 100. If students miss putting a 0 in the quotient, they will find their answer to be radically off when they compare it to their estimate.

Another way to reinforce the importance of 0 is to write numbers on the board without 0s and ask if they make sense. For example, write "one hundred six" on the board as 16 (no 0, right?) or 1006 (too many 0s). This is just a fun way to remind students that 0 is a pretty important number when it comes to place value and writing numbers.

Name: _____   Date: _____

Which Has More?

Tape a piece of paper here
to cover the answer.

_____ × _____ = _____

Lift the flap for answers.

Tape a piece of paper here
to cover the answer.

_____ × _____ = _____

Lift the flap for answers.

Name: _____   Date: _____

WORD PROBLEM

WORD PROBLEM

Amanda had 5 bags of marbles with 3 marbles in each.
Brad had 4 bags of marbles with 4 marbles in each. Who had more marbles?

BASICS BOX

Multiplication is like repeated addition, but faster. We can solve this problem by adding, but since the groups are equal it is easier to multiply.

Amanda $5 \times 3 = 15$ marbles

OOOOO
OOOOO
OOOOO

Brad $4 \times 4 = 16$ marbles

OOOO
OOOO
OOOO
OOOO

Brad has more.

$$5 \quad \times \quad 3 \quad = \quad 15$$
factor   factor   product

PRACTICE

Rewrite each addition sentence as a multiplication fact.

1. $2 + 2 + 2 + 2 =$ _____ × _____ = _____

2. $3 + 3 + 3 =$ _____ × _____ = _____

3. $4 + 4 =$ _____ × _____ = _____

4. $5 + 5 + 5 + 5 =$ _____ × _____ = _____

5. $1 + 1 + 1 + 1 =$ _____ × _____ = _____

6. $6 + 6 + 6 =$ _____ × _____ = _____

7. $5 + 5 + 5 + 5 + 5 + 5 =$ _____ × _____ = _____

8. Rewrite the multiplication fact as repeated addition.

   $4 \times 7 =$ _____ + _____ + _____ + _____ = _____

JOURNAL

Give an example of how knowing a multiplication fact is more efficient than repeated addition.

EXAMPLE

$6 \times 4 = ?$ OO OO OO OO OO OO
         $4 + 4 + 4 + 4 + 4 + 4 = 24$

Reteaching Math: Multiplication & Division © 2008 by Bob Krech, Scholastic Teaching Resources

Name: _____   Date: _____

Introducing Multiplication

Label the parts of this equation.

1. 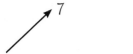 7   ×   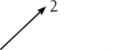 2   =   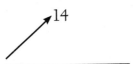 14

    _____   _____   _____

Write a multiplication fact to match each addition sentence.

2. 9 + 9 + 9 + 9 + 9 = _____ × _____ = _____

3. 5 + 5 + 5 + 5 + 5 = _____ × _____ = _____

4. 7 + 7 = _____ × _____ = _____

5. 3 + 3 + 3 + 3 + 3 + 3 + 3 = _____ × _____ = _____

6. 2 + 2 + 2 = _____ × _____ = _____

7. 4 + 4 + 4 + 4 + 4 = _____ × _____ = _____

8. 8 + 8 + 8 = _____ × _____ = _____

Write the repeated addition that matches each multiplication fact.

9. 2 × 5 = _____ + _____ = _____

10. 5 × 2 = _____ + _____ + _____ + _____ + _____ = _____

11. 7 × 3 = _____ + _____ + _____ + _____ + _____ + _____ + _____ = _____

12. 6 × 7 = _____ + _____ + _____ + _____ + _____ + _____ = _____

13. Joe has 7 boxes with 5 pencils in each box. How many pencils does he have? _____

14. Robin earned $5 every day for 8 days. How much money did she earn? _____

Ricardo Cardenza, President

Cardenza Collector Card and Coin Company

Dear Class:

Allow me to introduce myself. My name is Ricardo Cardenza. I am the president of the Cardenza Collector Card and Coin Company. My company manufactures interesting and unusual collector cards and coins. We make cards for a variety of sports (like hockey) and other topics (such as animals of the rainforest) and coins featuring the presidents.

We have to use a lot of math to keep track of our ordering, printing, and billing. We were hoping to get some help from you as we have been very busy.

If you could begin by helping with my card display plans, I'd greatly appreciate it. We have to arrange the cards in interesting ways for our customers. We put them in arrays (like arrangements). For example, if we have 4 cards we might arrange them these ways:

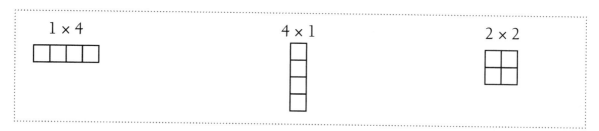

I have used multiplication sentences to describe the arrays. We have to try a variety of arrays. In fact, we have to try to find all of them—at least all of the ones that use single-digit numbers since our boxes can't hold more than 9 cards in width or length. Please find the arrays and multiplication facts that describe them for these amounts: 1, 2, 3, 4, 5, 6, 7, 8, 9, 10, 12, 14, 15, 16, 18, 20, 21, 24, 25, 27, 28, 30, 32, 35, 36, 40, 42, 45, 48, 49, 54, 56, 63, 64, 72, 81.

Please help by completing the enclosed Arrays Chart. Thank you very much for your help.

Sincerely,

Ricardo Cardenza

Reteaching Math: Multiplication & Division © 2008 by Bob Krech, Scholastic Teaching Resources

Name: _____   Date: _____

Arrays Chart

Color in the squares below to show all of the possible arrays for your assigned products. Write the multiplication facts that describe each array. Do not use double-digit numbers.

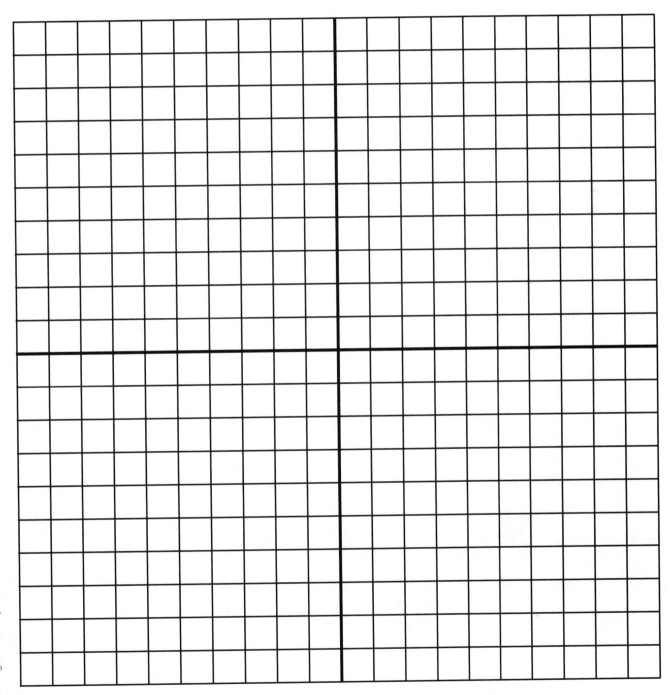

Reteaching Math: Multiplication & Division © 2008 by Bob Krech, Scholastic Teaching Resources

Name: _____ Date: _____

Samantha opened a box of candy and saw 8 rows of candy with 6 candies in each row. How many candies were in the box?

BASICS BOX

An array is an arrangement of objects. In math we often arrange items in rows (horizontal) and columns (vertical). Here's an array of Samantha's candy box:

We could write this as a repeated addition sentence: 6 + 6 + 6 + 6 + 6 + 6 + 6 + 6 = _____ , which we could read as 8 groups of 6. We can add up the 6s, count the candies in the array, or, if we memorize the fact, we know that 8 x 6 = 48 candies.

PRACTICE

Write the multiplication fact for each array.

1.

_____ × _____ = _____

2.

_____ × _____ = _____

3.

_____ × _____ = _____

4.

_____ × _____ = _____

Draw the array for each multiplication fact, then find the product.

5. 3 x 2 = _____

6. 4 x 3 = _____

7. 2 x 9 = _____

8. 9 x 2 = _____

JOURNAL

Give an example of how knowing a multiplication fact is more efficient than repeated addition.

Reteaching Math: Multiplication & Division © 2008 by Bob Krech, Scholastic Teaching Resources

Name: _____   Date: _____

Multiplication Arrays

Write the multiplication fact for each array.

1. ⬚⬚⬚⬚⬚⬚⬚

_____ × _____ = _____

3. (array of circles, 4 rows × 5 columns)

_____ × _____ = _____

5. (array of circles, 3 rows × 2 columns)

_____ × _____ = _____

2. (array of squares, 2 rows × 2 columns)

_____ × _____ = _____

4. (column of 3 triangles)

_____ × _____ = _____

6. (array of circles, 2 rows × 3 columns)

_____ × _____ = _____

Draw the array for each multiplication fact, then find the product.

7. $8 \times 5 =$ _____

8. $2 \times 6 =$ _____

9. $4 \times 4 =$ _____

10. $3 \times 9 =$ _____

11. $7 \times 2 =$ _____

12. $2 \times 7 =$ _____

Review.

13. $5 + 5 =$ _____ × _____ = _____

14. $4 + 4 + 4 + 4 + 4 =$ _____ × _____ = _____

15. $2 + 2 + 2 + 2 =$ _____ × _____ = _____

16. $6 + 6 + 6 + 6 + 6 + 6 =$ _____ × _____ = _____

Label each circled number factor or product.

17. $3 \times ④ = 12$ _____

18. $⑨ \times 9 = 81$ _____

19. $8 \times 7 = ㊶$ _____

20. $㊾ = 7 \times 7$ _____

Reteaching Math: Multiplication & Division © 2008 by Bob Krech, Scholastic Teaching Resources

Ricardo Cardenza, President

Cardenza Collector Card and Coin Company

Dear Students:

In the work we have ahead, we will be using a lot of multiplication. To help you keep track of the multiplication strategies we will need to use, I am supplying you with our Math Secret page.

You should create your own handbook to keep all of the Math Secrets I will be revealing to you. These secrets are strategies mathematicians and businesspeople know and use quite a bit. Part of your training will be to learn all the 100 basic multiplication facts. This can be challenging at times, but I have great confidence in you, and I know the Math Secrets will help you immensely.

This first secret is very basic. It is called "Doubles." I would like you to complete the Doubles Math Secret page with your teacher. You should also complete the 100 Multiplication Facts Chart for Doubles. This chart will help you see how many of the facts a specific strategy can help you with.

Keep all of these secrets in a Math Secrets Handbook that you can use for reference as you continue your work with our company. Once again, I am very delighted to have your help.

Sincerely,

Ricardo Cardenza

Reteaching Math: Multiplication & Division © 2008 by Bob Krech, Scholastic Teaching Resources

Name: _____ Date: _____

Math Secret #_____

Strategy Name: _____

PICTURE EXAMPLE

WORDS _____

_____

_____

_____

_____

_____

EQUATION EXAMPLE

Reteaching Math: Multiplication & Division © 2008 by Bob Krech, Scholastic Teaching Resources

43

Name: _____   Date: _____

100 Multiplication Facts Chart

Strategy Name: _____

$\times$	0	1	2	3	4	5	6	7	8	9
0	0×0	0×1	0×2	0×3	0×4	0×5	0×6	0×7	0×8	0×9
1	1×0	1×1	1×2	1×3	1×4	1×5	1×6	1×7	1×8	1×9
2	2×0	2×1	2×2	2×3	2×4	2×5	2×6	2×7	2×8	2×9
3	3×0	3×1	3×2	3×3	3×4	3×5	3×6	3×7	3×8	3×9
4	4×0	4×1	4×2	4×3	4×4	4×5	4×6	4×7	4×8	4×9
5	5×0	5×1	5×2	5×3	5×4	5×5	5×6	5×7	5×8	5×9
6	6×0	6×1	6×2	6×3	6×4	6×5	6×6	6×7	6×8	6×9
7	7×0	7×1	7×2	7×3	7×4	7×5	7×6	7×7	7×8	7×9
8	8×0	8×1	8×2	8×3	8×4	8×5	8×6	8×7	8×8	8×9
9	9×0	9×1	9×2	9×3	9×4	9×5	9×6	9×7	9×8	9×9

Name: _____ Date: _____

Reteaching Math: Multiplication & Division © 2008 by Bob Krech, Scholastic Teaching Resources

WORD PROBLEM

Victor bought 2 packs of raccoon football cards.
There are 8 cards in each pack. How many cards did he have in all?

BASICS BOX

Multiplying by 2 is just like doubling a factor. Victor buys 2 packs of 8 cards:

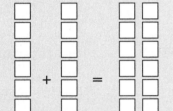

8 + 8 = 16

2 x 8 is the same as saying "2 groups of 8":

2 x 8 = 8 + 8 = 16

PRACTICE

Find the products. Draw pictures to prove your answer.

1. $7 \times 2 =$ _____

2. $2 \times 9 =$ _____

3. $4 \times 2 =$ _____

Match the multiplication fact with the addition sentence that means the same.

4. $4 \times 2 =$ _____

    a. 4 + 2

    b. 2 + 2 + 2 + 2

    c. 2 + 2

    d. 8 + 2

5. $2 \times 9 =$ _____

    a. 9 + 2

    b. 9 + 9

    c. 18 – 9

    d. 11 + 9

JOURNAL

Can you use doubles to solve 2 x 100? Explain your answer.

Name: _____   Date: _____

Doubles Strategy for Multiplication

Find the products.

1. $2 \times 9 =$ _____

2. $7 \times 2 =$ _____

3. $2 \times 2 =$ _____

4. $9 \times 2 =$ _____

5. $5 \times 2 =$ _____

6. $2 \times 4 =$ _____

7. $8 \times 2 =$ _____

8. $2 \times 8 =$ _____

Draw a picture to show each multiplication fact, then find the product.

9. $4 \times 2 =$ _____

10. $2 \times 3 =$ _____

Double each number.

11. 3 _____

12. 7 _____

13. 4 _____

14. 8 _____

15. 2 _____

Match each multiplication fact with the addition sentence that means the same.

16. $7 \times 2 =$

  a. $2 + 2 + 2 + 2 + 2 + 2 + 2$

  b. $7 + 2$

  c. $9 + 0$

  d. $5 + 2$

17. $2 \times 4 =$

  a. $4 + 2$

  b. $6 + 2$

  c. $4 + 4$

  d. $1 + 1 + 1 + 1 + 1 + 1 + 1 + 1$

Reteaching Math: Multiplication & Division © 2008 by Bob Krech, Scholastic Teaching Resources

Ricardo Cardenza, President
Cardenza Collector Card and Coin Company

Dear Students:

I'm sure you've heard about the new sports craze that's sweeping the nation: Insect Basketball! Cardenza Cards and Coins is celebrating this wonderful new sport by issuing a series of cards featuring famous Insect Basketball players.

Because there are 5 starting players on a basketball team, these cards will come in packs of 5. We need to figure out how many cards there'll be in every Insect Basketball multipack. Your teacher will explain how we pack the multipacks. After you practice your packing, please complete the order table below so that we can ship these cards right away!

	Insect Basketball Multipacks			
	Number of 5-packs in a multipack	Number of cards in each pack	Multiplication fact	How many cards in a multipack?
1.	0	5	0 x 5	0
2.	1	5	1 x 5	
3.	2	5	2 x 5	
4.	3	5		
5.	4	5		
6.	5	5		
7.	6	5	6 x 5	30
8.	7	5		
9.	8	5		
10.	9	5		

Sincerely,

Ricardo Cardenza

P.S. Don't forget to add this new Math Secret to your handbook!

Reteaching Math: Multiplication & Division © 2008 by Bob Krech, Scholastic Teaching Resources

Name: _____   Date: _____

One Hundred Chart

1	2	3	4	5	6	7	8	9	10
11	12	13	14	15	16	17	18	19	20
21	22	23	24	25	26	27	28	29	30
31	32	33	34	35	36	37	38	39	40
41	42	43	44	45	46	47	48	49	50
51	52	53	54	55	56	57	58	59	60
61	62	63	64	65	66	67	68	69	70
71	72	73	74	75	76	77	78	79	80
81	82	83	84	85	86	87	88	89	90
91	92	93	94	95	96	97	98	99	100

Name: _____ Date: _____

WORD PROBLEM

Akhila bought 7 packs of Insect Basketball cards. There are 5 cards in a pack. How many cards did she get in all?

BASICS BOX

In this problem, you need to find out how many cards are in 7 groups of 5, or 7 x 5. You can multiply by fives in different ways.

1. On your fingers

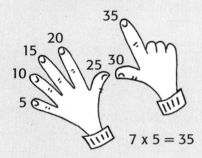

7 x 5 = 35

2. Making tens

10 + 10 + 10 + 5 = 35

| 10 | 10 | 10 | 5 |

3. Using a friendly fact

I know 5 x 5 = 25, plus 2 more fives = 35

PRACTICE

Find the products.

1.   7
    ×   5

2.   5
    ×   2

3.   9
    ×   5

4.   5
    ×   9

5.   5
    ×   0

6. 4 × 5 = _____

7. 5 × 8 = _____

8. 3 × 5 = _____

9. 6 × 5 = _____

10. 5 × 1 = _____

JOURNAL

What bigger multiplication problem can you solve using your fives facts? Explain how your basic fives facts help you solve the tougher problem.

Reteaching Math: Multiplication & Division © 2008 by Bob Krech, Scholastic Teaching Resources

Name: _____   Date: _____

Fives Facts for Multiplication

Find the products.

1. $9 \times 5 =$ _____

2. $5 \times 3 =$ _____

3. $4 \times 5 =$ _____

4. $5 \times 7 =$ _____

5. $2 \times 5 =$ _____

6. $5 \times 8 =$ _____

7. $5 \times 1 =$ _____

8. $8 \times 5 =$ _____

9. $5 \times 0 =$ _____

10. $6 \times 5 =$ _____

Draw a picture to show each multiplication fact, then find the product.

11. $3 \times 5 =$ _____

12. $5 \times 2 =$ _____

Review.

13. $\begin{array}{r} 1 \\ \times\ 2 \\ \hline \end{array}$

14. $\begin{array}{r} 2 \\ \times\ 9 \\ \hline \end{array}$

15. $\begin{array}{r} 7 \\ \times\ 2 \\ \hline \end{array}$

16. $\begin{array}{r} 2 \\ \times\ 8 \\ \hline \end{array}$

17. $\begin{array}{r} 9 \\ \times\ 2 \\ \hline \end{array}$

18. $\begin{array}{r} 2 \\ \times\ 0 \\ \hline \end{array}$

19. $\begin{array}{r} 2 \\ \times\ 1 \\ \hline \end{array}$

20. $\begin{array}{r} 3 \\ \times\ 2 \\ \hline \end{array}$

Ricardo Cardenza, President
Cardenza Collector Card and Coin Company

Dear Students:

We just finished cleaning our card-printing machines. We have a huge factory and lots of machines. Every once in a while, we have to shut down sections of the factory to clean out cards when they get stuck in the machines.

Our machine supervisors kept a chart of our recent cleanup. They marked down which section of the factory the machines are located in and how many machines are in that section. They also recorded how many cards were stuck in each machine. Here's their chart below. Could you find how many cards were stuck in each section and figure out how many cards were stuck altogether? Thanks for your help!

Machine Cleaning Chart			
	Number of machines in section	Cards stuck in each machine	Total cards in section
Building #1			
Section A	5	1	
Section B	3	0	
Section C	8	1	
Building #2			
Section D	1	5	
Section E	8	0	
Section F	4	1	
Building #3			
Section G	1	3	
Section H	3	1	
Section I	9	0	
		Grand Total	

Sincerely,

Ricardo Cardenza

Name: _____   Date: _____

Zach has 8 boxes, with 1 Cardenza Company collector coin in each box.
How many coins does he have?
Rahul has 8 empty coin boxes. How many coins does he have?

BASICS BOX

Multiplying by 0.
Rahul has 8 groups of nothing—which is still nothing.

$$8 \times 0 = 0$$

Any number multiplied by 0 is 0.

Multiplying by 1.
Zach has 8 groups of 1 coin.

◯◯◯◯◯◯◯◯

$$8 \times 1 = 8 \text{ coins}$$

Any number times 1 equals the number you started with!

JOURNAL

What is 4,127 x 0?
Explain your answer.
What is 654 x 1?
How do you know?

PRACTICE

Find the products.

1. $0 \times 9 =$ _____

2. $1 \times 8 =$ _____

3. $0 \times 1 =$ _____

4. $6 \times 1 =$ _____

5. $7 \times 0 =$ _____

6. $2 \times 1 =$ _____

7. $3 \times 1 =$ _____

8. $0 \times 0 =$ _____

9. $1 \times 6 =$ _____

10. $9 \times 1 =$ _____

11. $\begin{array}{r} 7 \\ \times\ 0 \\ \hline \end{array}$

12. $\begin{array}{r} 1 \\ \times\ 1 \\ \hline \end{array}$

13. $\begin{array}{r} 5 \\ \times\ 0 \\ \hline \end{array}$

14. $\begin{array}{r} 0 \\ \times\ 1 \\ \hline \end{array}$

15. $\begin{array}{r} 4 \\ \times\ 1 \\ \hline \end{array}$

16. $\begin{array}{r} 1 \\ \times\ 9 \\ \hline \end{array}$

Name: _____ Date: _____

Zeros and Ones Facts for Multiplication

Find the products.

1. $\begin{array}{r} 1 \\ \times\ 2 \\ \hline \end{array}$

2. $\begin{array}{r} 9 \\ \times\ 1 \\ \hline \end{array}$

3. $\begin{array}{r} 0 \\ \times\ 8 \\ \hline \end{array}$

4. $\begin{array}{r} 6 \\ \times\ 0 \\ \hline \end{array}$

5. $\begin{array}{r} 4 \\ \times\ 1 \\ \hline \end{array}$

6. $\begin{array}{r} 1 \\ \times\ 7 \\ \hline \end{array}$

7. $1 \times 0 =$ _____

8. $0 \times 3 =$ _____

9. $3 \times 1 =$ _____

10. $4 \times 0 =$ _____

Draw a picture to show each multiplication fact, then find the product.

11. $1 \times 9 =$ _____

12. $1 \times 5 =$ _____

13. $1 \times 6 =$ _____

14. $6 \times 1 =$ _____

15. $2 \times 1 =$ _____

16. $1 \times 4 =$ _____

Review.

17. $\begin{array}{r} 9 \\ \times\ 5 \\ \hline \end{array}$

18. $\begin{array}{r} 5 \\ \times\ 2 \\ \hline \end{array}$

19. $\begin{array}{r} 2 \\ \times\ 8 \\ \hline \end{array}$

20. $\begin{array}{r} 8 \\ \times\ 5 \\ \hline \end{array}$

21. $3 \times 2 =$ _____

22. $4 \times 5 =$ _____

23. $9 \times 2 =$ _____

24. $2 \times 5 =$ _____

Reteaching Math: Multiplication & Division © 2008 by Bob Krech, Scholastic Teaching Resources

Ricardo Cardenza, President
Cardenza Collector Card and Coin Company

Dear Students:

I've just received the latest order for our newest cards. These are custom-made starting-team baseball cards. As you know, a baseball team has 9 players on the field at a time during a game. The players who begin the game for a team are known as "the starting nine" or the "starters." We are making these new sets of cards for Little League teams. So far we have orders from quite a few leagues in the forest area. Can you complete the order chart for us? Thanks!

Forest Little League Baseball Cards			
League	Number of teams	Number of cards per team	Total number of cards
1. Muskrats	3	9	
2. Skunks	1	9	
3. Porcupines	2	9	
4. Squirrels	9	9	
5. Field Mice	4	9	
6. Raccoons	7	9	
7. Opossums	6	9	
8. Buzzards	5	9	
9. Otters	8	9	
10. Trees	0	9	
11. Sparrows	10	9	

How many cards do we need to print altogether?

Sincerely,

Ricardo Cardenza

Name: _____ Date: _____

Tony pitched 6 complete games this season. Each game was 9 innings long. How many innings did Tony pitch this season?

BASICS BOX

The Nifty Nines strategy is based on two interesting patterns that occur when multiplying by 9.

First, if we add the digits of the product, they always equal 9. Second, the first digit of the product is 1 less than the factor being multiplied by 9.

In Tony's problem, we multiply 9 x 6. Since 5 is 1 less than 6, we know the product begins with a 5. To make the product's digits add up to 9, we would have to add 4. So the product of 9 x 6 is 54. Tony pitched 54 innings this season.

EXAMPLE

Susan read 9 pages in the encyclopedia every night for 5 days. How many pages did she read all together?

$9 \times 5 = ?$

One less than 5 is 4.

$4 + 5 = 9$, so the product is 45.

PRACTICE

Find the products.

1.
$$\begin{array}{r} 9 \\ \times\ 9 \\ \hline \end{array}$$

2.
$$\begin{array}{r} 3 \\ \times\ 9 \\ \hline \end{array}$$

3.
$$\begin{array}{r} 5 \\ \times\ 9 \\ \hline \end{array}$$

4. $9 \times 2 =$ _____

5. $7 \times 9 =$ _____

6. $9 \times 0 =$ _____

7. $1 \times 9 =$ _____

8. $9 \times$ _____ $= 72$

9.   _____ $\times 9 = 36$

JOURNAL

Explain how you could use the Nifty Nines strategy to find the answer to 8 x 9.

Name: _____   Date: _____

Nifty Nines Strategy for Multiplication

Find the products.

1. $9 \times 6 =$ _____

2. $9 \times 1 =$ _____

3. $9 \times 9 =$ _____

4. $8 \times 9 =$ _____

5. $9 \times 8 =$ _____

6. $0 \times 9 =$ _____

7.
$$\begin{array}{r} 2 \\ \times \ \square \\ \hline 18 \end{array}$$

8.
$$\begin{array}{r} 9 \\ \times \ \square \\ \hline 27 \end{array}$$

9.
$$\begin{array}{r} 9 \\ \times \ \square \\ \hline 45 \end{array}$$

10.
$$\begin{array}{r} 9 \\ \times \ 4 \\ \hline \end{array}$$

11.
$$\begin{array}{r} 6 \\ \times \ 9 \\ \hline \end{array}$$

12.
$$\begin{array}{r} 7 \\ \times \ 9 \\ \hline \end{array}$$

Review.

13.
$$\begin{array}{r} 5 \\ \times \ 4 \\ \hline \end{array}$$

14.
$$\begin{array}{r} 8 \\ \times \ 5 \\ \hline \end{array}$$

15.
$$\begin{array}{r} 5 \\ \times \ 5 \\ \hline \end{array}$$

16.
$$\begin{array}{r} 2 \\ \times \ 8 \\ \hline \end{array}$$

17.
$$\begin{array}{r} 7 \\ \times \ 2 \\ \hline \end{array}$$

18.
$$\begin{array}{r} 0 \\ \times \ 8 \\ \hline \end{array}$$

19.
$$\begin{array}{r} 1 \\ \times \ 4 \\ \hline \end{array}$$

Write the multiplication fact that matches the picture.

20. _____ × _____ = _____

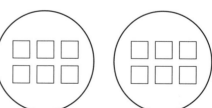

Ricardo Cardenza, President
Cardenza Collector Card and Coin Company

Dear Mathematicians:

Do you enjoy doubling numbers? I sure do, especially when those numbers are profits. And so, we at Cardenza Card and Coin Company have decided to DOUBLE the size of our Ostrich Racing card packs (formerly sold in packs of 2). Yes, you read it here first. Your favorite Ostrich Racing trading cards will now be available in packs of 4! Hard to believe, isn't it?

Of course, this from-two-to-four business means one thing: We need your multiplication skills! Please complete the diagrams for our factory's brand-new Double-Doubler Machines. You'll need to double your factors and then double them again to show how the machines will work.

Your twos facts and regular doubling skills will serve you well, so get cracking on this double-doubling—on the double-double!

Sincerely,

Ricardo Cardenza

Name: _____ Date: _____

Double-Doubler Machines

Double-double the factors to complete the fours facts.

| 3 | | 6 | 12 | | 3 x 4 = 12 |
| Factor | | Double | Double-Double | | Fact |

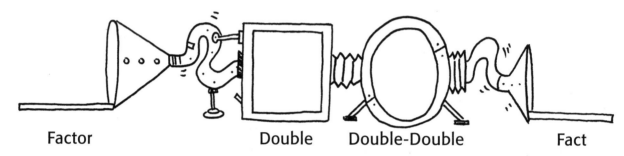

| Factor | Double | Double-Double | Fact |

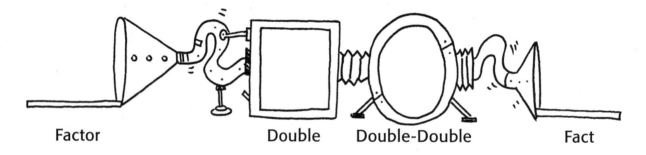

| Factor | Double | Double-Double | Fact |

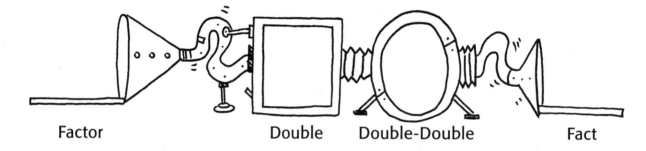

| Factor | Double | Double-Double | Fact |

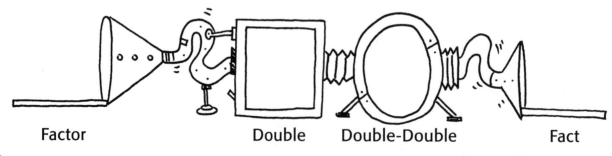

| Factor | Double | Double-Double | Fact |

58

Reteaching Math: Multiplication & Division © 2008 by Bob Krech, Scholastic Teaching Resources

Name: _____   Date: _____

Wendy collected 4 packs of Hamster Rodeo cards. There are 6 cards in each pack. How many cards did she have in all?

BASICS BOX

To find the product of a fours fact, double the other factor you're multiplying. Then double it again.

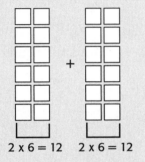

2 x 6 = 12   2 x 6 = 12

In 4 x 6, double 6 to make 12, and then double that number to get the product:

4 x 6 = 24

PRACTICE

Solve by double-doubling.

1. 4 x 7 = _____

Double 7 = _____

Double again = _____

2. 4 x 9 = _____

Double 9 = _____

Double again = _____

Find the products.

3. 4 x 3 = _____

4. 5 x 4 = _____

5. 1 x 4 = _____

6. 8 x 4 = _____

7. 4 x 8 = _____

8. 7 x 4 = _____

9. $\begin{array}{r} 4 \\ \times\ 9 \\ \hline \end{array}$

10. $\begin{array}{r} 6 \\ \times\ 4 \\ \hline \end{array}$

11. $\begin{array}{r} 4 \\ \times\ 2 \\ \hline \end{array}$

12. $\begin{array}{r} 4 \\ \times\ 7 \\ \hline \end{array}$

JOURNAL

Can you use Double-Doubling to solve 25 x 4? How?

Name: _____   Date: _____

Double-Double Four Facts

Find the products.

1. $\begin{array}{r} 8 \\ \times\ 4 \\ \hline \end{array}$

2. $\begin{array}{r} 9 \\ \times\ 4 \\ \hline \end{array}$

3. $\begin{array}{r} 3 \\ \times\ 4 \\ \hline \end{array}$

4. $\begin{array}{r} 4 \\ \times\ 2 \\ \hline \end{array}$

5. $\begin{array}{r} 0 \\ \times\ 4 \\ \hline \end{array}$

6. $\begin{array}{r} 4 \\ \times\ 9 \\ \hline \end{array}$

Complete the table.

	Number	Double	Double Again
7.		8	
8.	8		
9.	3	6	
10.			36
11.		12	
12.	5		

Draw a picture to show each multiplication fact, then find the product.

13. $5 \times 4 =$ _____

14. $4 \times 3 =$ _____

Review.

15. $\begin{array}{r} 9 \\ \times\ 0 \\ \hline \end{array}$

16. $\begin{array}{r} 1 \\ \times\ 8 \\ \hline \end{array}$

17. $\begin{array}{r} 2 \\ \times\ 6 \\ \hline \end{array}$

18. $\begin{array}{r} 4 \\ \times\ 2 \\ \hline \end{array}$

19. $\begin{array}{r} 2 \\ \times\ 0 \\ \hline \end{array}$

20. $\begin{array}{r} 2 \\ \times\ 9 \\ \hline \end{array}$

21. $\begin{array}{r} 1 \\ \times\ 3 \\ \hline \end{array}$

22. $\begin{array}{r} 3 \\ \times\ 0 \\ \hline \end{array}$

23. $\begin{array}{r} 1 \\ \times\ 9 \\ \hline \end{array}$

24. $\begin{array}{r} 3 \\ \times\ 9 \\ \hline \end{array}$

Reteaching Math: Multiplication & Division © 2008 by Bob Krech, Scholastic Teaching Resources

Ricardo Cardenza, President
Cardenza Collector Card and Coin Company

Dear Students:

They say that good things come in threes—and the new Cardenza Card and Coin Company's Lawn Chairs of Antarctica collectible coins prove that this is true. Yes, for a small cost, you can be the proud owner of a complete set of 3 coins celebrating only the most memorable pieces of lawn furniture from that coldest of continents.

Naturally, we expect these new coins will sell fast, so we need your help in organizing our coin warehouse. I really admire the work you've done in class with doubles. You really know your doubling facts. Please use the Doubles-Plus-One Math Secret method, which is custom-made for threes facts, and help us plan our next shipment of 3-coin packs.

How many Lawn Chairs of Antarctica coin sets will be in each box? Draw pictures to show how you doubled and then added one more set.

1. 6 sets of 3 coins

3. 5 sets of 3 coins

2. 9 sets of 3 coins

4. 8 sets of 3 coins

Three times your friend,

Ricardo Cardenza

Name: _____   Date: _____

Justin bought 3 sets of Lawn Chairs of Antarctica coins.
There are 8 coins in each set. How many coins did Justin buy in all?

BASICS BOX

To use the Double-Plus-One strategy when multiplying by 3, double the other factor you're multiplying. Then add one more of that factor.

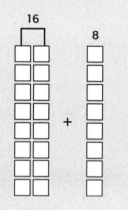

16 + 8 = 24

So to multiply 3 x 8, first double 8 to get 16. Then add one more group of 8:

16 + 8 = 24

PRACTICE

Solve by using Double-Plus-One. Draw a picture to show how you used Double-Plus-One for each fact.

1.   3 x 7 = _____

2.   6 x 3 = _____

Find the products.

3.   4 x 3 = _____

4.   9 x 3 = _____

5.   3 x 5 = _____

6.   8 x 3 = _____

7.   2 x 3 = _____

8.   3 x 2 = _____

JOURNAL

Write a poem about multiplying by 3.
Draw a picture to illustrate your poem.

Reteaching Math: Multiplication & Division © 2008 by Bob Krech, Scholastic Teaching Resources

Name: _____ Date: _____

Using a Double-Plus-One Strategy with Threes Facts

Find the products.

1. $0 \times 3 =$ _____

2. $3 \times 9 =$ _____

3. $3 \times 2 =$ _____

4. $6 \times 3 =$ _____

5. $3 \times 8 =$ _____

6. $1 \times 3 =$ _____

Complete the table.

	Number	Double	Number + Double
	4	8	12
7.	6		
8.		16	
9.		14	
10.			18
11.	9		
12.			15

Draw a picture that shows each multiplication fact, then find the product.

13. $3 \times 4 =$ _____

14. $1 \times 3 =$ _____

Review.

15. $4 \times 8 =$ _____

16. $9 \times 2 =$ _____

17. $7 \times 4 =$ _____

18. $5 \times 3 =$ _____

19. $\begin{array}{r} 8 \\ \times\ 0 \\ \hline \end{array}$

20. $\begin{array}{r} 6 \\ \times\ 4 \\ \hline \end{array}$

21. $\begin{array}{r} 9 \\ \times\ 7 \\ \hline \end{array}$

22. $\begin{array}{r} 5 \\ \times\ 2 \\ \hline \end{array}$

23. $\begin{array}{r} 4 \\ \times\ 8 \\ \hline \end{array}$

24. $\begin{array}{r} 9 \\ \times\ 1 \\ \hline \end{array}$

Reteaching Math: Multiplication & Division © 2008 by Bob Krech, Scholastic Teaching Resources

Ricardo Cardenza, President

Cardenza Collector Card and Coin Company

Dear Students:

I'm so honored to have your help and so glad that you've been working hard on learning your multiplication facts. You're going to need those strong multiplication skills now because our work is becoming more challenging.

To help you with the toughest facts—the sixes, sevens, and eights facts—I have arranged for you to receive official Cardenza Company training, with our best Math Secrets yet.

The first of these Super Math Secrets is the Friendly Chunks strategy. Today, I want you to learn this new Super Strategy and use it to calculate a special card order for us. These facts use the biggest factors on the times table, but I believe that your smart solving and our advanced strategy will make you expert toughie solvers.

Use your Friendly Chunks Strategy to complete this order!

	Order	Friendly Chunk Facts	Final Product
Toughie Card Packs			
1.	7 packs of 8 cards	$3 \times 8 = 24$ and $4 \times 8 = 32$	$24 + 32 = 56$
2.	6 packs of 9 cards		
3.	8 packs of 7 cards		
4.	9 packs of 8 cards		
5.	7 packs of 9 cards		
6.	6 packs of 7 cards		

Happy Toughie-zapping,

Ricardo Cardenza

Reteaching Math: Multiplication & Division © 2008 by Bob Krech, Scholastic Teaching Resources

Name: _____ Date: _____

WORD PROBLEM

Tom bought 7 packs of Collectible Vegetable cards. There are 8 cards in each pack.
How many cards did Tom buy in all?

BASICS BOX

You can solve tricky facts by putting your groups into Friendly Chunks. To solve 7 x 8, take 7 groups of 8:

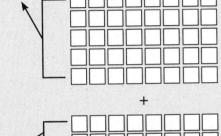

5 x 8 = 40

+

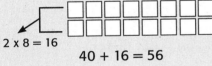

2 x 8 = 16

40 + 16 = 56

Find easier facts in your tough fact:

5 groups of 8 = 40

2 groups of 8 = 16

Add these products together:

40 + 16 = 56

7 x 8 = 56

PRACTICE

Solve using Friendly Chunks. Draw a picture to show how you made Friendly Chunks.

1. $8 \times 7 =$ _____

2. $7 \times 6 =$ _____

Find the products.

3. $9 \times 4 =$ _____

4. $6 \times 9 =$ _____

5. $7 \times 4 =$ _____

6. $7 \times 8 =$ _____

7. $\begin{array}{r} 8 \\ \times\ 8 \\ \hline \end{array}$

8. $\begin{array}{r} 7 \\ \times\ 5 \\ \hline \end{array}$

9. $\begin{array}{r} 8 \\ \times\ 6 \\ \hline \end{array}$

10. $\begin{array}{r} 9 \\ \times\ 8 \\ \hline \end{array}$

JOURNAL

What are the easiest facts to use for Friendly Chunks?

Name: _____   Date: _____

Friendly Chunks Strategy
for Sixes, Sevens, and Eights Facts

1. To solve 7 × 8, I can use these Friendly Facts:

Fact: _____ × _____ = ◯   AND   Fact: _____ × _____ = ◯

◯ + ◯ = _____

7 × 8 = _____

2. To solve 8 × 6, I can use these Friendly Facts:

Fact: _____ × _____ = ◯   AND   Fact: _____ × _____ = ◯

◯ + ◯ = _____

8 × 6 = _____

Draw a picture to show each fact. Circle the Friendly Facts. Add your products.

Example: 7 × 6 = ?

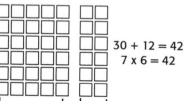

30 + 12 = 42
7 × 6 = 42

5 x 6 = 30   2 x 6 = 12

3. 8 × 7 = _____

4. 6 × 9 = _____

Review.

5. 9 × 8 = _____

6. 4 × 9 = _____

7. 2 × 7 = _____

8. 4 × 0 = _____

9. 5 × 8 = _____

10. 6 × 9 = _____

11. 6 × 5 = _____

12. 4 × 4 = _____

13. 1 × 1 = _____

14. 0 × 2 = _____

15. 7 × 1 = _____

16. 5 × 4 = _____

Reteaching Math: Multiplication & Division © 2008 by Bob Krech, Scholastic Teaching Resources

Ricardo Cardenza, President
Cardenza Collector Card and Coin Company

Dear Students:

Congratulations on doing so well with Friendly Chunks! Now you're ready to learn the next Cardenza Advanced Math Secret: Half-Then-Double!

The important thing to remember about this advanced strategy is that it will work only on facts with at least one even number. Your doubling skills will help you here, so be ready to use them.

Practice with your teacher, then fill in the order table below using the Half-Then-Double strategy to figure out how many cards we need to send to our customers.

	Order	Half that many sets	Double that number	Final product
	Half-Then-Double Strategy			
	8 packs of 7 cards	4 packs of 7 cards = 28 cards	28 + 28 = 56	8 x 7 = 56
1.	6 packs of 9 cards			
2.	4 packs of 9 cards			
3.	8 packs of 8 cards			
4.	6 packs of 8 cards			
5.	8 packs of 9 cards			

Happy Halving and Delightful Doubling,

Ricardo Cardenza

Name: _____ Date: _____

Almost-a-Sport Card Order Form

Ever hear of Ping-Pong Ball Hockey or Beachball Baseball? Of course you have! Cardenza Collector Card and Coin Company has released Almost-a-Sport Card Packs in honor of these "almost sports." Fill out this order form using "almost facts" to help you solve each fact. The idea is to use similar facts you already know to help you solve the more difficult fact. See the first example below.

	Order	I can use this Almost Fact to solve this fact	Number of cards
	8 packs of 7 cards	7 packs of 7 cards = 49, plus one more pack	8 x 7 = 56
1.	9 packs of 8 cards		
2.	8 packs of 6 cards		
3.	6 packs of 9 cards		
4.	6 packs of 7 cards		
5.	7 packs of 8 cards		
6.	9 packs of 7 cards		

Almost-a-Sport Card Packs

Reteaching Math: Multiplication & Division © 2008 by Bob Krech, Scholastic Teaching Resources

Name: _____   Date: _____

Luis collected 8 packs of Parakeet Soccer Legends cards.
There are 7 cards in each pack. How many cards are there in all?

BASICS BOX

Luis can use Half-Then-Double to solve this problem.

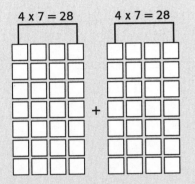

4 x 7 = 28   4 x 7 = 28

He has 8 groups of 7.
4 groups of 7 is 28.
28 + 28 = 56

8 x 7 = 56

PRACTICE

Use Half-Then-Double to solve the following problems. Draw a picture to show how you used the strategy.

1.   6 × 7 = _____

2.   8 × 6 = _____

JOURNAL

Can you use Half-Then-Double to solve 6 x 15? How?

Name: _____ Date: _____

Half-Then-Double Strategy
for Sixes, Sevens, and Eights Facts

Complete the table.

	Fact	Half as Many Groups	Double Your Product
	8×6	$4 \times 6 = 24$	48
1.	4×9		
2.	6×8		
3.	6×9		
4.	8×3		
5.	6×5		
6.	8×8		
7.	6×7		
8.	8×5		

Find the products.

9. $4 \times 8 =$ _____

10. $8 \times 3 =$ _____

11. $6 \times 5 =$ _____

12. $8 \times 7 =$ _____

13. $4 \times 9 =$ _____

14. $8 \times 6 =$ _____

15. $6 \times 7 =$ _____

16. $8 \times 8 =$ _____

17. $9 \times 3 =$ _____

18. $8 \times 7 =$ _____

Review.

19. $5 \times 8 =$ _____

20. $2 \times 9 =$ _____

21. $7 \times 1 =$ _____

22. $8 \times 0 =$ _____

23. $2 \times 4 =$ _____

24. $1 \times 2 =$ _____

25. $3 \times 9 =$ _____

26. $8 \times 8 =$ _____

27. $4 \times 7 =$ _____

28. $5 \times 0 =$ _____

29. $8 \times 6 =$ _____

30. $7 \times 7 =$ _____

70

Reteaching Math: Multiplication & Division © 2008 by Bob Krech, Scholastic Teaching Resources

Ricardo Cardenza, President
Cardenza Collector Card and Coin Company

Dear Students:

We are getting ready to offer our newest product—Mammal Collector Coins. We have planned the first set of mammals. There are 35 coins. We are thinking about having collectors buy them in sets of 5. That would give us 7 sets to sell. We could also sell them in sets of 7. That would give us 5 sets.

Look at these other coin sets we are thinking about selling. How do you think we should arrange them for sale? Fill in the blanks on the chart to tell us at least two ways we could distribute them. Thank you.

	Set Type	Number of Coins in a Set	Number of Sets	Total Number of Coins
Mammal Collector Coins				
1.	Dogs			63
2.	Dogs			63
3.	Cats			35
4.	Cats			35
5.	Monkeys			72
6.	Monkeys			72
7.	Horses			21
8.	Horses			21
9.	Gerbils			15
10.	Gerbils			15

Thanks,

Ricardo Cardenza

Reteaching Math: Multiplication & Division © 2008 by Bob Krech, Scholastic Teaching Resources

Name: _____   Date: _____

WORD PROBLEM

Michelle bought 5 packs of 4 cards. Cassi bought 4 packs of 5 cards. Who has more cards?

BASICS BOX

It doesn't matter if you switch the factors around—the product will stay the same. This is called the Commutative Property of Multiplication. It means that 5 groups of 4 will equal 4 groups of 5.

Michelle and Cassi each have the same number of cards: 20.

PRACTICE

How many arrays can you draw to show each product?

1.   12

2.   20

JOURNAL

How can you prove that 4 x 9 = 9 x 4 without using numbers? Explain your answer.

Reteaching Math: Multiplication & Division © 2008 by Bob Krech, Scholastic Teaching Resources

Name: _____   Date: _____

Commutative Property

Fill in the missing factors and find the products.

1. $2 \times$ _____ $= 3 \times$ _____ $=$ _____

2. $6 \times$ _____ $= 9 \times$ _____ $=$ _____

3. $7 \times$ _____ $= 8 \times$ _____ $=$ _____

4. $3 \times$ _____ $= 8 \times$ _____ $=$ _____

5. $5 \times$ _____ $= 4 \times$ _____ $=$ _____

6. $4 \times$ _____ $= 7 \times$ _____ $=$ _____

Draw dots inside the circles to complete the pictures.

Example:

7.

8.

9.

10.

Review.

11.
$$\begin{array}{r} 9 \\ \times\ 8 \\ \hline \end{array}$$

12.
$$\begin{array}{r} 7 \\ \times\ 5 \\ \hline \end{array}$$

13.
$$\begin{array}{r} 4 \\ \times\ 8 \\ \hline \end{array}$$

14.
$$\begin{array}{r} 3 \\ \times\ 7 \\ \hline \end{array}$$

15.
$$\begin{array}{r} 2 \\ \times\ 0 \\ \hline \end{array}$$

16.
$$\begin{array}{r} 6 \\ \times\ 4 \\ \hline \end{array}$$

17.
$$\begin{array}{r} 3 \\ \times\ 4 \\ \hline \end{array}$$

18.
$$\begin{array}{r} 0 \\ \times\ 8 \\ \hline \end{array}$$

19. $8 \times 2 =$ _____

20. $3 \times 9 =$ _____

21. $7 \times 3 =$ _____

22. $1 \times 9 =$ _____

23. $8 \times 0 =$ _____

24. $5 \times 7 =$ _____

25. $4 \times 3 =$ _____

26. $2 \times 4 =$ _____

27. $0 \times 2 =$ _____

28. $6 \times 1 =$ _____

29. $8 \times 3 =$ _____

30. $7 \times 9 =$ _____

31. $6 \times 7 =$ _____

32. $4 \times 4 =$ _____

Reteaching Math: Multiplication & Division © 2008 by Bob Krech, Scholastic Teaching Resources

Ricardo Cardenza, President
Cardenza Collector Card and Coin Company

Dear Students:

Big! Bigger! Um, even bigger! That's how I'm thinking about this next set of coins we're producing—Famous Umbrellas of the 20th Century!

I started with a set of 1 coin. I figured that could be the Big set. Then I figured, okay, for the Bigger set, I'd put in 10 coins! Then for the Even Bigger set—hang on to your desks—100 coins!

Here are the orders so far:

	Orders	Set Size	Total Coins
1.	3	Big	
2.	3	Bigger	
3.	3	Even Bigger	
4.	6	Big	
5.	6	Bigger	
6.	6	Even Bigger	

Famous Umbrellas of the 20th Century Coin Sets

I'm suspecting there must be a pattern here, so we won't have to use a calculator with some of these bigger numbers. What do you think? Please figure this out.

Thanks,

Ricardo Cardenza

Reteaching Math: Multiplication & Division © 2008 by Bob Krech, Scholastic Teaching Resources

Name: _____ Date: _____

WORD PROBLEM

Tanvi was selling boxes of candy. Each box had 6 pieces of candy in it.
The first week she sold 10 boxes. The second week she visited an apartment building
where she sold 100 boxes. How many pieces of candy did she sell in all?

BASICS BOX

There are place-value patterns in multiplication that can help you multiply by 10s, 100s, or even 1,000s. This is great for saving time by using mental math.

1. Begin by finding the simple fact in the larger problem. This is 6 x 1, which is 6.

2. Count the 0s in the problem. In this case, there is one. This lets us know there will be one 0 in the product.

3. Write 6 with one 0 behind it to get the product of 60. Repeat the same three steps for the second part to get a product of 600.

In Tanvi's problem, we have to multiply 6 x 10 for the first week, which is 60. The second week is 6 x 100 = 600. Add 600 and 60 to see that she sold 660 pieces of candy.

PRACTICE

Find the products.

1. $5 \times 10 =$ _____

2. $5 \times 100 =$ _____

3. $5 \times 1,000 =$ _____

4. $10 \times 3 =$ _____

5. $10 \times 30 =$ _____

6. $10 \times 300 =$ _____

7. $500 \times 4 =$ _____

8. $50 \times 4 =$ _____

9. $40 \times 50 =$ _____

10. $2 \times 20 =$ _____

11. $2 \times 200 =$ _____

12. $20 \times 20 =$ _____

JOURNAL

How can multiplication patterns help you solve a problem like 16 x 100?

Reteaching Math: Multiplication & Division © 2008 by Bob Krech, Scholastic Teaching Resources

Name: _____   Date: _____

Multiplication Patterns

Find the products.

1. $10 \times 8 =$ _____

2. $10 \times 80 =$ _____

3. $100 \times 8 =$ _____

4. $1,000 \times 8 =$ _____

5. $4 \times 40 =$ _____

6. $400 \times 40 =$ _____

7. $1 \times 400 =$ _____

8. $40 \times 40 =$ _____

9. $9 \times 10 =$ _____

10. $90 \times 10 =$ _____

11. $9 \times 20 =$ _____

12. $90 \times 20 =$ _____

13. $900 \times 20 =$ _____

14. $20 \times 50 =$ _____

15. $200 \times 50 =$ _____

Review.

16. What strategy could be used to solve 8×6? Explain.

17. What property of multiplication tells us that if $3 \times 9 = 27$ then $9 \times 3 = 27$?

18. Give an example of a fact for the Half-Then-Double strategy.

Reteaching Math: Multiplication & Division © 2008 by Bob Krech, Scholastic Teaching Resources

Ricardo Cardenza, President
Cardenza Collector Card and Coin Company

Reteaching Math: Multiplication & Division © 2008 by Bob Krech, Scholastic Teaching Resources

Dear Students:

I need your help figuring out some new orders for some great coin sets. Here are the three wonderful sets:

Famous Furniture Coins – This set includes 6 coins: sleeper sofa, kitchen table, dining room table, coffee table, couch, and kitchen chair.

Awesome Appliance Coins – This set includes 8 coins: stove, oven, refrigerator, washer, dryer, microwave, vacuum cleaner, and dishwasher.

Incredible Ice Cream Flavor Coins – This set includes 9 coins: vanilla, chocolate, strawberry, cookie dough, coffee, pistachio, mint chocolate chip, banana, and peanut butter.

Here are the latest orders:

	Number of Orders	Coin Set	Total Coins
Great Coin Sets			
1.	17 sets	Furniture	
2.	18 sets	Appliances	
3.	25 sets	Ice Cream	

Grand total _____

What is the total number of coins for each set? What is the grand total of all the coins we have to make? Thanks as always for your help.

Sincerely,

Ricardo Cardenza

Name: _____   Date: _____

Ray bought 7 packs of juice boxes for the class picnic.
There were 24 juice boxes in a pack. How many juice boxes did Ray buy?

BASICS BOX

There are many methods for multiplying
numbers with more than one digit. Here are
two that Ray (and you) can use:

Traditional	**Partial Products**
24	24
x 7	x 7
Multiply ones	Multiply ones
24	4
x 7	x 7
28	28
Regroup 2 tens	Multiply tens
2	20
24	x 7
x 7	140
8	
Multiply tens	Add both products
2	140
24	+ 28
x 7	168 juice boxes
8	
2 x 7 = 14 + 2 = 16	
24	
x 7	
168 juice boxes	

PRACTICE

Solve each problem using both
methods. Show your work.

1.
```
   36
 ×  8
_____
```

2.
```
   52
 ×  9
_____
```

JOURNAL

Which multiplication method do you
find easiest to work with? Why?

Reteaching Math: Multiplication & Division © 2008 by Bob Krech, Scholastic Teaching Resources

Name: _____   Date: _____

Multiplication Methods

Find the products. Show your work.

1.   13
       × 4
    _____

2.   25
       × 3
    _____

3.   50
       × 7
    _____

4.   68
       × 6
    _____

5.   93
       × 5
    _____

6.   41
       × 8
    _____

7.   33
       × 3
    _____

8.   76
       × 2
    _____

Review.

9. 30 × 50 = _____

10. 300 × 50 = _____

11. 40 × 80 = _____

12. 400 × 800 = _____

Reteaching Math: Multiplication & Division © 2008 by Bob Krech, Scholastic Teaching Resources

79

Ricardo Cardenza, President
Cardenza Collector Card and Coin Company

Dear Students:

We've got an interesting situation on our hands right now. We've got a lot of leftover coins in our storage area so we want to try to sell them in sets.

We figure we could sell them in different-size sets with a good discount on the price. We plan to sell small sets of 3 coins, medium sets of 5 coins, large sets of 8 coins, and jumbo sets of 10 coins.

The chart below shows how many coins of each type we have. Help us figure out how many sets of each type of coins we can make.

	Coins	Number of Coins	Type of Set	How many sets can we make?
	Leftover Coins			
1.	Mixed Sports	25	medium	
2.	Famous Furniture	50	medium	
3.	Lizards	24	large	
4.	Wizards	24	small	
5.	Dogs	100	jumbo	
6.	Cats	64	large	
7.	Weeds	27	small	

Thanks for your help!

Sincerely,

Ricardo Cardenza

Reteaching Math: Multiplication & Division © 2008 by Bob Krech, Scholastic Teaching Resources

Find-the-Multiplication-Card Game

7 x 7	5 x 3	4 x 2	9 x 6	2 x 8	1 x 5
8 x 4	7 x 5	3 x 9	6 x 2	4 x 4	7 x 8
3 x 8	5 x 2	7 x 2	3 x 4	9 x 5	6 x 8
49 ÷ 7	15 ÷ 5	8 ÷ 2	54 ÷ 9	16 ÷ 8	5 ÷ 1
32 ÷ 4	35 ÷ 5	27 ÷ 3	12 ÷ 6	16 ÷ 4	56 ÷ 7
24 ÷ 8	10 ÷ 2	14 ÷ 7	12 ÷ 3	45 ÷ 9	48 ÷ 8

Name: _____ Date: _____

WORD PROBLEM

Maria has 4 friends coming over. She has a package of 20 cookies to share with them. How many cookies should each child, including Maria, get if they all share fairly?

BASICS BOX

Division is an operation that helps us to share an amount into equal groups. It is the opposite of multiplication. Multiplication helps us understand, solve, and even check division problems.

Maria has 20 cookies. She has to divide them among 5 people. We could solve with a picture:

We can write an equation like this:

divisor → $5)\overline{20}$ OR $20 \div 5 = ?$

dividend   dividend   divisor

If we think about division with multiplication we think $20 \div 5 =$ ___ is the same as $5 \times$ ___ $= 20$. We see that since $5 \times 4 = 20$ then $20 \div 5 = 4$. So each child would get 4 cookies.

PRACTICE

Find the quotients.

1. $18 \div 2 =$ _____

2. $12 \div 6 =$ _____

3. $42 \div 6 =$ _____

4. $9)\overline{27}$

5. $3)\overline{24}$

6. $5)\overline{45}$

JOURNAL

What multiplication fact would help you solve $56 \div 8 = ?$

Reteaching Math: Multiplication & Division © 2008 by Bob Krech, Scholastic Teaching Resources

Name: _____   Date: _____

Introducing Division: One-Digit Divisors Without Remainders

Find the quotients.

1. $1\overline{)9}$

8. $20 \div 4$ _____

2. $6\overline{)48}$

9. $8\overline{)64}$

3. $6 \div 6 =$ _____

10. $6\overline{)36}$

4. $21 \div 7 =$ _____

11. $28 \div 7 =$ _____

5. $5\overline{)30}$

12. $14 \div 2 =$ _____

6. $3\overline{)15}$

13. $8\overline{)56}$

7. $9 \div 3 =$ _____

14. $5\overline{)25}$

Review.

15. $3 \times 8 =$ _____

18. $25 \times 10 =$ _____

16. $7 \times 6 =$ _____

19. $50 \times 50 =$ _____

17. $4 \times 20 =$ _____

20. $500 \times 50 =$ _____

Reteaching Math: Multiplication & Division © 2008 by Bob Krech, Scholastic Teaching Resources

Ricardo Cardenza, President
Cardenza Collector Card and Coin Company

Dear Students:

I'm having a little problem. I seem to have a lot of packs of Favorite Socks of All Time cards left over. Why, I don't know. I thought they would sell out overnight.

As a reward to my loyal employees in the factory, I decided to give these cards to the workers who run the presses the cards were printed on. I want to give each worker a fair share of the cards, but I'm having trouble because the numbers are not coming out even. Actually, the first one for Press A did come out even, and I filled in the chart. But the rest are a problem. Help!

	Printing Press	Number of Cards	Number of Workers	Cards for Each Worker	Leftovers
	A	25	5	5	0
1.	B	30	5		
2.	C	30	4		
3.	D	45	8		
4.	E	71	8		
5.	F	100	6		
6.	G	100	5		
7.	H	127	7		

Favorite Socks of All Time Cards

As always, thanks for your help.

Sincerely,

Ricardo Cardenza

Reteaching Math: Multiplication & Division © 2008 by Bob Krech, Scholastic Teaching Resources

I-Want-Remainders Game

36	40	30	22	29	27
19	28	49	34	35	12
17	23	51	25	20	32
16	48	15	46	47	56
44	31	18	37	45	39
81	54	26			
33	52	63			
4	5	6			
7	8	9			

Spinner sections: 4, 5, 9, 6, 8, 7

Reteaching Math: Multiplication & Division © 2008 by Bob Krech, Scholastic Teaching Resources

Name: _____   Date: _____

WORD PROBLEM

Max is putting eggs into cartons. He has 27 eggs. Each carton holds 6 eggs.
How many cartons will he fill? Will there be any eggs left over?

BASICS BOX

Sometimes when we divide we don't end up with completely equal groups. We have extras or leftovers. These extras are called the *remainder.*

Max has 27 eggs. If he puts them in containers of 6, it would look like this.

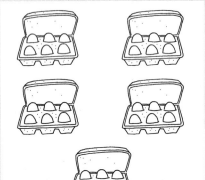

We see he can fill 4 cartons, but he will have 3 extra eggs.

$$\begin{array}{r} 4\ r3 \\ 6\overline{)27} \\ 24 \\ \hline 3 \end{array}$$ → This is how we write the remainder.

Remember: The remainder should always be less than the divisor.

PRACTICE

Find the quotients.

1. $4\overline{)23}$

2. $5\overline{)27}$

3. $6\overline{)47}$

4. $2\overline{)13}$

5. $4\overline{)15}$

6. $3\overline{)26}$

7. $8\overline{)79}$

8. $4\overline{)29}$

JOURNAL

List and explain all the steps for dividing 17 by 3.

Reteaching Math: Multiplication & Division © 2008 by Bob Krech, Scholastic Teaching Resources

Name: _____ Date: _____

Single-Digit Divisors with Remainders

Find the quotients.

1. $2\overline{)19}$

2. $5 \div 2 =$ _____

3. $20 \div 6 =$ _____

4. $7\overline{)55}$

5. $4\overline{)19}$

6. $37 \div 6 =$ _____

7. $50 \div 8 =$ _____

8. $8\overline{)49}$

9. $8\overline{)26}$

10. $66 \div 7 =$ _____

11. $8 \div 5 =$ _____

12. $6\overline{)34}$

13. $8\overline{)45}$

14. $23 \div 5 =$ _____

Review.

15. $16 \div 4 =$ _____

16. $54 \div 9 =$ _____

17. $30 \times 3 =$ _____

18. $11 \times 6 =$ _____

19. $125 \times 10 =$ _____

20. $60 \times 100 =$ _____

Ricardo Cardenza, President
Cardenza Collector Card and Coin Company

Dear Students:

Sorry to share more bad news, but Favorite Fruit Commemorative Coins have not been the big sellers we'd hoped. We've got great coins, like Papaya, Mango, Grapefruit, and all of the classics. I don't understand the poor sales, but that's the way it is.

Since we've got a lot left, we're going to be giving them away as a bonus to people who order our Little League Team cards. Little Leaguers like fruit, right? Now, I've got to figure out how many coins to give to each team. Assistance, please!

	Team	Number of Coins	Number of Players	Coins per Player	Leftovers
1.	Ocelots	124	11		
2.	Skunks	143	16		
3.	Lemurs	436	4		
4.	Wombats	88	11		
5.	Pythons	124	17		
6.	Toads	205	15		
7.	Beetles	109	13		

Favorite Fruit Commemorative Coins

Thanks,

Ricardo Cardenza

Reteaching Math: Multiplication & Division © 2008 by Bob Krech, Scholastic Teaching Resources

Name: _____   Date: _____

Causing-Problems Game

| Dividend | ÷ | Divisor | = | Quotient | r | Remainder |

| Dividend | ÷ | Divisor | = | Quotient | r | Remainder |

✂ -

6	8	10	12	14	3
3	2	1	4	3	18
1	4	6	8	10	12
14	16	20	7	9	24
2	3	1	4	6	20

Name: _____ Date: _____

For the Little League Banquet, 12 players put out 360 place settings. How many places did each player have to set?

BASICS BOX

Dividing with a 2-digit divisor follows the same basic steps as with a 1-digit divisor.

$$12\overline{)360}$$

We can't divide 3 by 12 so we look to the tens and see 36.

$$\begin{array}{r} 3 \\ 12\overline{)360} \end{array}$$

We can divide 36 by 12 because 12 x 3 = 36.

$$\begin{array}{r} 30 \\ 12\overline{)360} \\ \underline{36} \\ 00 \end{array}$$

Try to find the multiplication fact that gets you as close as possible.

EXAMPLE

$$16\overline{)112}$$

Here we can't divide the hundreds by 16, or even the tens, so we have to look all the way to the ones—that's the whole number. We have to try out some multiplication that will bring us close or right on 112.

16 x 5 = 80	No
16 x 6 = 96	No
16 x 7 = 112	Yes!

PRACTICE

Find the quotients.

1. $25\overline{)100}$ 6. $26\overline{)858}$

2. $25\overline{)250}$ 7. $18\overline{)828}$

3. $16\overline{)208}$ 8. $17\overline{)356}$

4. $35\overline{)630}$ 9. $39\overline{)786}$

5. $31\overline{)682}$ 10. $12\overline{)422}$

JOURNAL

How is dividing by a one-digit divisor different from dividing by a two-digit divisor? Give an example with your explanation.

Reteaching Math: Multiplication & Division © 2008 by Bob Krech, Scholastic Teaching Resources

Name: _____   Date: _____

Dividing by Two-Digit Divisors

Find the quotients.

1. 15)‾300‾

2. 11)‾99‾

3. 13)‾117‾

4. 15)‾60‾

5. 23)‾529‾

6. 35)‾210‾

7. 12)‾324‾

8. 15)‾945‾

9. 13)‾858‾

10. 20)‾300‾

11. 23)‾874‾

12. 21)‾735‾

13. 42)‾546‾

14. 45)‾1,620‾

Review.

15. 8)‾24‾

16. 8)‾240‾

17. 5)‾271‾

18. 39 ÷ 6 = _____

Name: _____ Date: _____

Ricardo Cardenza, President
Cardenza Collector Card and Coin Company

Dear Students:

Hooray! We are finally making some money! I never would have thought it, but do you know what's finally selling for us? Baseball cards! Just plain old baseball cards of professional baseball teams, like the Yankees and the Dodgers. Sound boring? Certainly not as exciting as Weeds of the World Collector Cards! Well, live and learn.

Thank you so much for all your help! Your multiplication and division skills really saved the day for me. All of our wonderful products, like Tremendous Teeth Cards and Fabulous Fruit Coins, would be sitting on shelves collecting dust, unsold, if it weren't for you.

I hope you have enjoyed working with us as much as we have enjoyed working with you. Best of luck in your mathematical and coin-and-card-collecting futures. Thank you again!

Three times your friend,

Ricardo Cardenza

P.S. Attached is a very valuable collector card as a special thank-you!

Reteaching Math: Multiplication & Division © 2008 by Bob Krech, Scholastic Teaching Resources

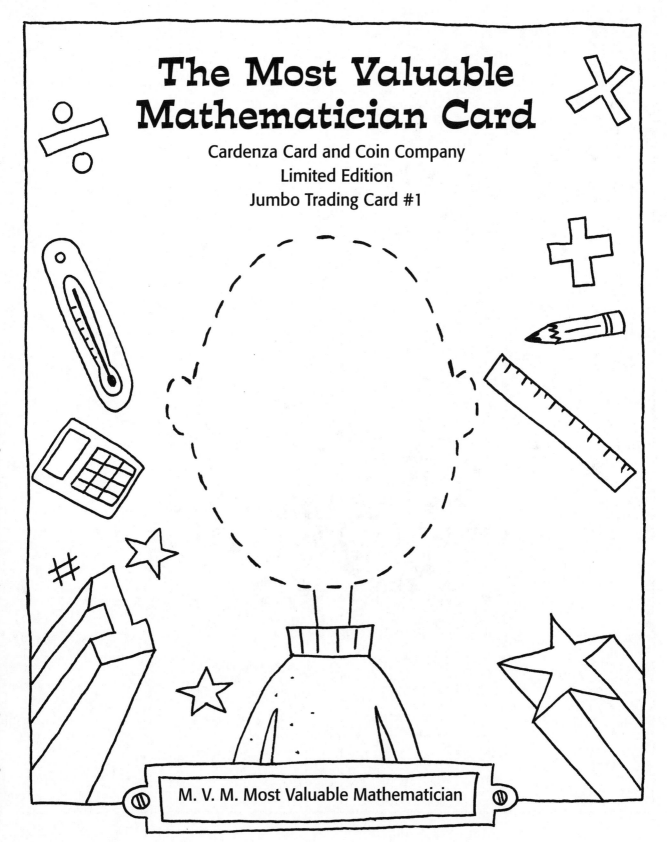

The Most Valuable Mathematician Card

Cardenza Card and Coin Company
Limited Edition
Jumbo Trading Card #1

M. V. M. Most Valuable Mathematician

Reteaching Math: Multiplication & Division © 2008 by Bob Krech, Scholastic Teaching Resources

Practice Page #1 (p. 36)
1. 4 × 2 = 8
2. 3 × 3 = 9
3. 2 × 4 = 8
4. 4 × 5 = 20
5. 4 × 1 = 4
6. 3 × 6 = 18
7. 6 × 5 = 30
8. 7 + 7 + 7 + 7 = 28
Journal: Answers will vary.

Review Page #1 (p. 37)
1. factor, factor, product
2. 5 × 9 = 45
3. 5 × 5 = 25
4. 2 × 7 = 14
5. 7 × 3 = 21
6. 3 × 2 = 6
7. 5 × 4 = 20
8. 3 × 8 = 24
9. 5 + 5 = 10
10. 2 + 2 + 2 + 2 + 2 = 10
11. 3 + 3 + 3 + 3 + 3 + 3 + 3 = 21
12. 7 + 7 + 7 + 7 + 7 + 7 = 42
13. 7 × 5 = 35 pencils
14. $5 × 8 = $40

Letter #2 (p. 38)
1 = 1 × 1
2 = 2 × 1, 1 × 2
3 = 3 × 1, 1 × 3
4 = 4 × 1, 1 × 4, 2 × 2
5 = 5 × 1, 1 × 5
6 = 6 × 1, 1 × 6, 3 × 2, 2 × 3
7 = 7 × 1, 1 × 7
8 = 8 × 1, 1 × 8, 4 × 2, 2 × 4
9 = 9 × 1, 1 × 9, 3 × 3
10 = 5 × 2, 2 × 5
12 = 6 × 2, 2 × 6, 3 × 4, 4 × 3
14 = 7 × 2, 2 × 7
15 = 3 × 5, 5 × 3
16 = 8 × 2, 2 × 8, 4 × 4
18 = 9 × 2, 2 × 9, 3 × 6, 6 × 3
20 = 4 × 5, 5 × 4
21 = 7 × 3, 3 × 7
24 = 6 × 4, 4 × 6, 3 × 8, 8 × 3
25 = 5 × 5
27 = 9 × 3, 3 × 9
28 = 7 × 4, 4 × 7
30 = 6 × 5, 5 × 6
32 = 8 × 4, 4 × 8
35 = 7 × 5, 5 × 7
36 = 9 × 4, 4 × 9, 6 × 6
40 = 5 × 8, 8 × 5
42 = 7 × 6, 6 × 7
45 = 9 × 5, 5 × 9
48 = 6 × 8, 8 × 6
49 = 7 × 7
54 = 9 × 6, 6 × 9
56 = 7 × 8, 8 × 7
63 = 9 × 7, 7 × 9

64 = 8 × 8
72 = 9 × 8, 8 × 9
81 = 9 × 9

Practice Page #2 (p. 40)
1. 3 × 4 = 12
2. 3 × 3 = 9
3. 4 × 5 = 20
4. 2 × 6 = 12
5. 6
6. 12
7. 18
8. 18
Journal: Answers will vary.

Review Page #2 (p. 41)
1. 1 × 7 = 7
2. 2 × 2 = 4
3. 4 × 5 = 20
4. 3 × 1 = 3
5. 3 × 2 = 6
6. 2 × 3 = 6
7. 40
8. 12
9. 16
10. 27
11. 14
12. 14
13. 2 × 5 = 10
14. 5 × 4 = 20
15. 4 × 2 = 8
16. 6 × 6 = 36
17. factor
18. factor
19. product
20. product

Practice Page #3 (p. 45)
1. 14
2. 18
3. 8
4. b
5. b
Journal: Answers will vary.

Review Page #3 (p. 46)
1. 18
2. 14
3. 4
4. 18
5. 10
6. 8
7. 16
8. 16
9. 8; pictures will vary.
10. 6; pictures will vary.
11. 6
12. 14
13. 8
14. 16
15. 4
16. a
17. c

Letter #4 (p. 47)
1. 0 × 5 = 0
2. 1 × 5 = 5
3. 2 × 5 = 10
4. 3 × 5 = 15
5. 4 × 5 = 20
6. 5 × 5 = 25
7. 6 × 5 = 30
8. 7 × 5 = 35
9. 8 × 5 = 40
10. 9 × 5 = 45

Practice Page #4 (p. 49)
1. 35
2. 10
3. 45
4. 45
5. 0
6. 20
7. 40
8. 15
9. 30
10. 5
Journal: Answers will vary.

Review Page #4 (p. 50)
1. 45
2. 15
3. 20
4. 35
5. 10
6. 40
7. 5
8. 40
9. 0
10. 30

11. 15; pictures will vary.
12. 10; pictures will vary.
13. 2
14. 18
15. 14
16. 16
17. 18
18. 0
19. 2
20. 6

Letter #5 (p. 51)
1. 5 × 1 = 5
2. 3 × 0 = 0
3. 8 × 1 = 8
4. 1 × 5 = 5
5. 8 × 0 = 0
6. 4 × 1 = 4
7. 1 × 3 = 3
8. 3 × 1 = 3
9. 9 × 0 = 0
Grand total: 28

Practice Page #5 (p. 52)
1. 0
2. 8
3. 0
4. 6
5. 0
6. 2
7. 3
8. 0
9. 6
10. 9
11. 0
12. 1
13. 0
14. 0
15. 4
16. 9
Journal: Answers will vary.

Review Page #5 (p. 53)
1. 2
2. 9
3. 0
4. 0
5. 4
6. 7
7. 0
8. 0
9. 3
10. 0
11. 9; pictures will vary.
12. 5; pictures will vary.
13. 6; pictures will vary.
14. 6; pictures will vary.
15. 2; pictures will vary.
16. 4; pictures will vary.
17. 45
18. 10
19. 16
20. 40

21. 6
22. 20
23. 18
24. 10

Letter #6 (p. 54)
1. 27
2. 9
3. 18
4. 81
5. 36
6. 63
7. 54
8. 45
9. 72
10. 0
11. 90
Total cards = 495

Practice Page #6 (p. 55)
1. 81
2. 27
3. 45
4. 18
5. 63
6. 0
7. 9
8. 8
9. 4
Journal: Answers will vary.

Review Page #6 (p. 56)
1. 54
2. 9
3. 81
4. 72
5. 72
6. 0
7. 9
8. 3
9. 5
10. 36
11. 54
12. 63
13. 20
14. 40
15. 25
16. 16
17. 14
18. 0
19. 4
20. $2 \times 6 = 12$

Practice Page #7 (p. 59)
1. 14, 28
2. 18, 36
3. 12
4. 20
5. 4
6. 32
7. 32
8. 28
9. 36

10. 24
11. 8
12. 28
Journal: Answers will vary.

Review Page #7 (p. 60)
1. 32
2. 36
3. 12
4. 8
5. 0
6. 36
7. 4, 16
8. 16, 32
9. 12
10. 9, 18
11. 6, 24
12. 10, 20
13. 20; pictures will vary.
14. 12; pictures will vary.
15. 0
16. 8
17. 12
18. 8
19. 0
20. 18
21. 3
22. 0
23. 9
24. 27

Letter #8 (p. 61)
1. $6 \times 3 = 18$
2. $9 \times 3 = 27$
3. $5 \times 3 = 15$
4. $8 \times 3 = 24$

Practice Page #8 (p. 62)
1. 21; pictures will vary.
2. 18; pictures will vary.
3. 12
4. 27
5. 15
6. 24
7. 6
8. 6
Journal: Answers will vary.

Review Page #8 (p. 63)
1. 0
2. 27
3. 6
4. 18
5. 24
6. 3
7. 12, 18
8. 8, 24
9. 7, 21
10. 6, 12
11. 18, 27
12. 5, 10
13. 12; pictures will vary.
14. 3; pictures will vary.

15. 32
16. 18
17. 28
18. 15
19. 0
20. 24
21. 63
22. 10
23. 32
24. 9

Letter #9 (p. 64)
Chunks will vary.
Final products:
1. 56
2. 54
3. 56
4. 72
5. 63
6. 42

Practice Page #9 (p. 65)
1. 56
2. 42
3. 36
4. 54
5. 28
6. 56
7. 64
8. 35
9. 48
10. 72
Journal: Answers will vary.

Review Page #9 (p. 66)
Chunks will vary.
Final products:
1. 56
2. 48
3. 56
4. 54
5. 72
6. 36
7. 14
8. 0
9. 40
10. 54
11. 30
12. 16
13. 1
14. 0
15. 7
16. 20

Letter #10 (p. 67)
1. 3 packs of 9 = 27;
   27 + 27 = 54;
   $6 \times 9 = 54$
2. 2 packs of 9 = 18;
   18 + 18 = 36;
   $4 \times 9 = 36$
3. 4 packs of 8 = 32;
   32 + 32 = 64;

   $8 \times 8 = 64$
4. 3 packs of 8 = 24;
   24 + 24 = 48;
   $6 \times 8 = 48$
5. 4 packs of 9 = 36;
   36 + 36 = 72;
   $8 \times 9 = 72$

**Activity: Almost-a-Sport
Card Order Form** (p. 68)
Almost Facts will vary.
Final products:
1. 72
2. 48
3. 54
4. 42
5. 56
6. 63

Practice Page #10 (p. 69)
Pictures will vary.
Final products:
1. 42
2. 48
Journal: Answers will vary.

Review Page #10 (p. 70)
1. $2 \times 9 = 18$; 36
2. $3 \times 8 = 24$; 48
3. $3 \times 9 = 27$; 54
4. $4 \times 3 = 12$; 24
5. $3 \times 5 = 15$; 30
6. $4 \times 8 = 32$; 64
7. $3 \times 7 = 21$; 42
8. $4 \times 5 = 20$; 40
9. 32
10. 24
11. 30
12. 56
13. 36
14. 48
15. 42
16. 64
17. 27
18. 56
19. 40
20. 18
21. 7
22. 0
23. 8
24. 2
25. 27
26. 64
27. 28
28. 0
29. 48
30. 49

Letter #11 (p. 71)
1. $9 \times 7 = 63$
2. $7 \times 9 = 63$
3. $7 \times 5 = 35$
4. $5 \times 7 = 35$

5. $9 \times 8 = 72$
6. $8 \times 9 = 72$
7. $7 \times 3 = 21$
8. $3 \times 7 = 21$
9. $5 \times 3 = 15$
10. $3 \times 5 = 15$

Practice Page #11 (p. 72)
1. Answers will vary.
2. Answers will vary.
Journal: The commutative property of multiplication proves that these equations have the same product and are equal because they have the exact same factors though in different orders.

Review Page #11 (p. 73)
1. 3, 2, 6
2. 9, 6, 54
3. 8, 7, 56
4. 8, 3, 24
5. 4, 5, 20
6. 7, 4, 28
7. (two circles, each with 4 dots)
8. (one circle with 5 dots)
9. (three circles, each with 3 dots)
10. (two circles, each with 9 dots)
11. 72
12. 35
13. 32
14. 21
15. 0
16. 24
17. 24
18. 0
19. 16
20. 27
21. 21
22. 9
23. 0
24. 35
25. 12
26. 8
27. 0
28. 6
29. 24
30. 63
31. 42
32. 16

Letter #12 (p. 74)
1. 3
2. 30
3. 300
4. 6
5. 60
6. 600

Practice Page #12 (p. 75)
1. 50
2. 500
3. 5,000
4. 30
5. 300
6. 3,000
7. 2,000
8. 200
9. 2,000
10. 40
11. 400
12. 400
Journal: Answers will vary.

Review Page #12 (p. 76)
1. 80
2. 800
3. 800
4. 8,000
5. 160
6. 16,000
7. 400
8. 1,600
9. 90
10. 900
11. 180
12. 1,800
13. 18,000
14. 1,000
15. 10,000
16. Answers will vary.
17. Commutative property
18. Answers will vary.

Letter #13 (p. 77)
1. 102
2. 144
3. 225
Grand total: 471 coins

Practice Page #13 (p. 78)
1. 288
2. 468
Journal: Answers will vary.

Review Page #13 (p. 79)
1. 52
2. 75
3. 350
4. 408
5. 465
6. 328
7. 99
8. 152
9. 1,500
10. 15,000

11. 3,200
12. 320,000

Letter #14 (p. 80)
1. 5
2. 10
3. 3
4. 8
5. 10
6. 8
7. 9

Practice Page #14 (p. 82)
1. 9
2. 2
3. 7
4. 3
5. 8
6. 9
Journal: $7 \times 8 = 56$ or $8 \times 7 = 56$

Review Page #14 (p. 83)
1. 9
2. 8
3. 1
4. 3
5. 6
6. 5
7. 3
8. 5
9. 8
10. 6
11. 4
12. 7
13. 7
14. 5
15. 24
16. 42
17. 80
18. 250
19. 2,500
20. 25,000

Letter #15 (p. 84)
1. 6, 0
2. 7, 2
3. 5, 5
4. 8, 7
5. 16, 4
6. 20, 0
7. 18, 1

Practice Page #15 (p. 86)
1. 5 r3
2. 5 r2
3. 7 r5
4. 6 r1
5. 3 r3
6. 8 r2
7. 9 r7
8. 7 r1
Journal: Answers will vary.

Review Page #15 (p. 87)
1. 9 r1
2. 2 r1
3. 3 r2
4. 7 r6
5. 4 r3
6. 6 r1
7. 6 r2
8. 6 r1
9. 3 r2
10. 9 r3
11. 1 r3
12. 5 r4
13. 5 r5
14. 4 r3
15. 4
16. 6
17. 90
18. 66
19. 1,250
20. 6,000

Letter #16 (p. 88)
1. 11, 3
2. 8, 15
3. 109, 0
4. 8, 0
5. 7, 5
6. 13, 10
7. 8, 5

Practice Page #16 (p. 90)
1. 4
2. 10
3. 13
4. 18
5. 22
6. 33
7. 46
8. 20 r16
9. 20 r6
10. 35 r2
Journal: Answers will vary.

Review Page #16 (p. 91)
1. 20
2. 9
3. 9
4. 4
5. 23
6. 6
7. 27
8. 63
9. 66
10. 15
11. 38
12. 35
13. 13
14. 36
15. 3
16. 30
17. 54 r1
18. 6 r3